CITYLIVING

CITYLIVING

INSPIRATIONAL HOMES IN THE HEART OF THE CITY

Contributing editors **Bo Niles** and **Katherine Sorrell**

RYLAND
PETERS
& SMALL
LONDON NEW YORK

First published in the USA in 2003 by
Ryland Peters & Small, Inc.
519 Broadway
5th Floor
New York, NY 10012
www.rylandpeters.com

10 9 8 7 6 5 4 3 2 1

Front jacket Joan Barnett's house in West
Hollywood, designed by William R. Hefner AIA,
interior design by Sandy Davidson Design; **back
jacket above left** Mrs. Venturini's apartment in
Milan; **above center** Evan Snyderman's house in
Brooklyn; **above right** Interior Designer Didier
Gomez's apartment in Paris; **below** Jonathan
Leitersdorf's apartment in New York designed by
Jonathan Leitersdorf/Just Design Ltd.

DESIGNER Luis Peral-Aranda
SENIOR EDITOR Henrietta Heald
PICTURE RESEARCHER Emily Westlake
PRODUCTION Patricia Harrington
ART DIRECTOR Gabriella Le Grazie
PUBLISHING DIRECTOR Alison Starling

Printed in China.

Library of Congress Cataloging-in-Publication Data

City living : inspirational homes in the heart of the city.
    p. cm.
Includes index.
  ISBN 1-84172-396-7
  1. Apartments. 2. Interior decoration. 3. City and town
life. I.
Title: Inspirational homes in the heart of the city.
  NK2195.A6 C57 2003
  747'.883'091732–dc21

                                        2002153693

CONTENTS

INTRODUCTION
by Bo Niles

Cities are as old as civilization itself. Embodying human hopes and dreams, they have long inspired artists, and it is through art that many of us visit a city a first time. For the rest of the world, after all, Tony Bennett left his heart in San Francisco, James Joyce is synonymous with Dublin, Marcel Proust and Emile Zola with Paris, Henry James and Edith Wharton with New York. A Roman Holiday is inconceivable without Audrey Hepburn. And then there's the tango in Buenos Aires, jazz in New Orleans, Amsterdam painted by Rembrandt. Each city is unique, true to itself and its inhabitants. And that is both its charm and its attraction.

OPPOSITE Many city dwellers yearn for the better quality of life traditionally associated with the countryside, and reminders of the rural idyll such as trees, plants, and wooden fences can be found in all sorts of unlikely urban settings—even in the shadows of Manhattan's water towers.

RIGHT The high-rise Barbican apartments in the City of London have an ancient Roman quality of robustness in their materials and detailing. The complex has become an icon of 1960s architecture.

Humans are, by nature, sociable creatures. Ever since our ancestors gave up a nomadic existence for a settled one based on trade and commerce, we have gathered in cities. In places as diverse and remote from each other as Mesopotamia and Egypt, China, South America—and, later, Greece and Rome—independent political units called city-states arose. Initially, these urban centers focused on the market square; soon, though, to protect themselves from jealous neighbors, cities girdled themselves with walls punctuated by ramparts, sentry towers, and gates.

By the Renaissance, many European cities had outgrown their defensive walls, and the economic-political structure was defined by nations rather than individual cities.

The next great transformation came about as a result of the Industrial Revolution and the new synergy of factory and railway. Historians of urban planning date the birth of the modern city to this time, when the invention of the machine, enabling mass-production of goods, supplanted individual ateliers and workshops as the primary source of income for many households.

From time immemorial, then, cities have been magnets for enterprise. The city connotes opportunity; for the thousands who still flock to them, cities hold out hope for a better life.

Cities are built not only of bricks and mortar (and, today, steel and glass), but also by reputation. Mention the name of a city—Paris, London, or Tokyo, say—and the mind's eye conjures up a specific vision of place. Every city has its own aura, its own energy, its own buzz. Each marches to its own heartbeat. Think of New Delhi. Shanghai. Stockholm. Bruges. Cape Town. How different each is from the other.

A city—yours or mine, anyone's—
wears its heart on its sleeve. And its
soul is present everywhere you turn.

Emblematic structures bring specific cities into focus. The Eiffel
Tower, Arc de Triomphe or Notre Dame and the Seine are Paris.
Big Ben, the Houses of Parliament, and St. Paul's are London. The
Empire State Building (and, tragically, the Twin Towers) say New
York. A Chinese junk sailing past a gleaming skyline says Hong
Kong; the Cristo on the mountaintop says Rio.

Every city, though, is more than the sum of its parts. In this era of
globalization and multiculturalism, few cities on earth have remained
homogenous. A city is the world in microcosm; neighborhoods are
worlds within that world. It can seem amazing that, in such a press
of humanity, one can see individuality everywhere—on a billboard or
road sign, in a store window or a cart propelled by a street vendor,
in the music drifting from the window of a passing taxi. In some
cities, hundreds of languages are spoken, hundreds of cultures
honored. In New York City's boroughs of Queens and Brooklyn,
for example, more than 100 languages are spoken.

Cities hearken to their own rhythms. Some operate 24/7,
adjusting to no perceptible circadian system at all. For inhabitants
of these continuously busy places, day may be night and night day,
either by choice or by necessity. The baker who rises long before
dawn passes the youthful reveler ambling home after a night of
clubbing. The subway bristles with passengers at every hour.

A city is marked not only by its tangible qualities, of course,
but also by subtler, ineffable ones: the way the sun falls across
a façade in the late afternoon, for example, or the way the rain
sparkles on cobblestones under the lamplight, how the wind
whistles through the streets, a smell of woodsmoke drifting from
a chimney top—or the pollution.

Even more than their counterparts in the
countryside, city homes are perceived as places
of refuge, havens from the cacophony of the
streets—as well as from the hustle and bustle
of a stressful work routine. Pods of privacy, city
apartments protect and soothe, even in a high-
rise that may be home to literally thousands of
like-minded souls.

For the most fortunate urbanites, the best
city apartments may embrace the essence of
nature and the countryside: long views into an
ever-changing sky, sunlight streaming in at the
window, gardens, and trees—even if they are
contained within the confines of a microscopic
backyard, terrace, or balcony. To city dwellers,
these attributes are priceless.

The dwelling places featured in the following
pages represent a variety of approaches to city
living. The first, Classic Elegance, captures the
soul of the city in its more traditional guise, with
accouterments recognizable at a glance that
symbolize a special sense of place. Streamlined
Sleek represents the style associated with loft
living—modernist or minimalist in mode, bold
and ultra-functional. Retro Redefined delves
into the recent past, when machine-made
furnishings, many originally conceived for office
interiors in the middle decades of 20th century,
made their comeback; today these pieces
are given pride of place in strikingly urbane
surroundings. And, last, Relaxed Eclectic offers
glimpses into homes whose hallmark is a quirky
self-expression as independent of spirit as the
personalities who inhabit them.

THIS PAGE AND
OPPOSITE Terraces,
balconies, and roof
gardens provide city
dwellers with access
to long views and big
skies, as well as giving
them the chance to
enjoy their own private
piece of outdoor space.

CLASSIC ELEGANCE

Most cities are defined as much by their architecture as by their urban plan. Commercial and residential buildings, old and new, espouse the values of the prevailing culture, be it indigenous or one that has moved in and set a new standard for design. As real estate agents' windows avow, certain areas of a city grow in value precisely because of the architectural quality of their buildings. In some cases, such as the home in Harlem, New York City, shown on pages 50–57, the renaissance of a neglected district can hinge on the grace of an architecturally noteworthy building. The tenant of this apartment moved in because he took pride in the provenance of his address—then made sure that interior modifications did not compromise the structure's integrity. Many people who live in classically elegant homes do not attempt to model their design on tradition. Instead, they introduce elements that appeal to them for intensely personal reasons—while acknowledging that they are preserving something precious of the urban fabric.

THEATRICAL SERENITY

A long time ago, the phrase "over the store" was used to describe the place where the shopkeeper lived, but it is now unusual for the rooms above shops to have any connection with what goes on downstairs. This building in Paris belonging to the versatile designer Philippe Model is an exception to the rule. Model uses the rooms above his store as a mixture of living space, entertaining suite, workshop, and background for photographing his creations. The apartment, which is full of architectural riches, lends itself entirely to theatricality in its role as an ever-changing background to work and play.

THIS PAGE The slightly uneven parquet flooring breaks up the light and provides a subtle raw umber background to the paint colors. Philippe Model likes to buy reproduction furniture rather than originals and then experiment with painting it, as he has done with the pieces seen in this room.

LEFT AND FAR LEFT
An accumulation of small decorative details makes Philippe Model's Paris apartment a place of varied visual enjoyment.

BELOW LEFT A doorway filled with panes of mirror glass creates an illusion of endless space and subtly modulated colors. The harlequin patchwork pillow is shorthand for the decorative philosophy of the apartment.

Paris has always been a city of apartments, and the grandest were traditionally found on the second floor of a house, arranged so that one room led into another, with a contrast between semi-public space at the front and more intimate rooms at the back. Philippe Model's building dates from the 17th century, with alterations in the 18th. It reflects the serene self-confidence of French taste during this period in its simple well-proportioned paneling, lightly touched with rococo decoration, and tall windows.

There are few modern conveniences here, even discreetly hidden from view. This is a romantic apartment, where the past comes to life, not in the manner of a museum with correct period items, but more as a stage set where feeling is more important than fact. Many of the mirrors that seductively enlarge the space are modern, distressed on the back to give a more flattering broken reflection.

Paint colors often start in odd places, running in a vertical line to a point not quite halfway across a panel, or creating a cubist effect of dissolving planes. Paneling such as this, broken into planes of different colors, frequently occurs as a background in many of the majestic late paintings of Georges Braque. Textiles are draped from ceiling to floor, and a kitchen in the oldest part of the house, stripped back to its wood frame, looks like the setting for a candlelit 17th-century scene.

Philippe Model loves experimenting with color and draws on a variety of historical inspirations to make new shapes.

Even if it is not authentic, this style of treating an old building has many benefits. It avoids the danger of stripping away all the layers of the past in an effort to turn the clock back to a past that can never really be recaptured, and may kill off the charm that has accumulated over centuries. Many people feel moved by the soft broken textures and the sense of hidden history

RIGHT Designing shoes is an important part of Model's work. Their presence adds a surreal touch to the rooms.

ABOVE The intricate Italian terrazzo tiling on the bathroom floor, resembling a mosaic, has been carefully preserved.

LEFT There are few modern conveniences in this apartment, where comfort takes second place to recapturing a sense of historical authenticity. In common with the other rooms, the bathroom features wood paneling, large mirrors, and painted walls and furniture. Traditional-style chrome fixtures in the shower complement the 19th-century zinc tub.

In this romantic apartment, the past comes to life, not in the manner of a museum, but more as a stage set, where feeling is more powerful than fact.

LEFT Daylight falling on crumpled, delicately patterned floral bedding creates its own form of rococo in the scene set by this distinctively French painted bed. The walls show ample evidence of experiments with paint, while the slightly uneven parquet flooring breaks up the light and creates a subtle raw umber background for the paint colors.

RIGHT An accumulation of small decorative details makes this Paris apartment a place of visual enjoyment.

that old houses acquire over time, but feel that, for everyday life, these oddities must be smoothed away. An interior like this is also a valid frame for creativity in the present, so that the building itself can be a sort of education, revealing secrets of its identity and personality over time to an attentive and imaginative owner. It also allows a creative interpenetration between past and present, and is an eye-opener as well as a delight for visitors. Philippe Model actually lives in another apartment in Paris; this one, apart from being a playground and studio, has introduced a wider circle of people to his design ideas. So many of them wanted to own copies of the items he made experimentally for his own use that he now sells a Philippe Model Maison line.

NOSTALGIC CHARM

This Milan apartment—while apparently sedate and perfectly normal, with its background of white-painted walls—offers as varied a collection of objects as one might expect to find in the kind of small local museum that has not rationalized its holdings. It does not matter much whether they are valuable or intrinsically beautiful, since they have been assembled to provide a stimulus for the eye and the imagination as well as to serve the functions of living.

LEFT The mixture of decorative textures in the floors and furniture, and in the pictures to the right of the doorway gives interest and a kind of consistency to the foyer space in this Milan apartment, suggesting exotic and distant places seen through the medium of a fairground.

BELOW A remarkable oval table in Art Nouveau style dominates the main sitting space.

Objects can act in the same way as the words of a language—not the sort of spoken and written language by which we hope to communicate exact meanings to each other, but one in which meanings are nevertheless produced by putting things side by side. The idea of the "amusing" object—which actually means an object that attracts attention by being placed deliberately out of context—would make an interesting study.

Probably most people never experience the urge to disorganize the world in this way, seeing their possessions as strictly functional or at least uncorrupted by duplicity or ambiguity of meaning, but, as the ancient Greeks realized in their earliest rules for making works of art, it is strangeness, not familiarity, that makes us think and feel emotion. "Amusing" objects may date back to the taste for oriental exotica in the 18th century, when the Chinese were seen by distant Europeans as magical, wise, and also rather comical. Surrealism in the 1930s was probably responsible for the 20th century's intermittent obsession with selecting the "wrong" things in a home—which for some people took on the importance of an artistic ideal.

The English art writer Adrian Stokes once described artists as "psychical removal men," bringing people's mental furniture out onto the sidewalk, where it could be displayed in all its oddity. Decorating with incongruity could be described as a reversal of this process, a kind of construction of a personal world through

THIS PAGE The use of a church pew as a room divider introduces the theme of pleasure in the ambiguity and dislocation of objects that runs through this apartment. The variety of wooden furniture echoes the fine parquet flooring.

RIGHT While the kitchen continues the theme of odd and unusual objects from the rest of the apartment, it has an airy lightness that provides a sense of wellbeing. The hanging light, adapted from an old kerosene lamp, is a particularly attractive piece, with its tendril-like brackets writhing up from the oil reservoir to the glass shade.

ABOVE The floor has the scattered, random quality of old terrazzo that evokes traditional Italian housekeeping and home cooking.

LEFT Old-fashioned kitchen equipment often has a strong sense of personality in its design. Even this refrigerator looks like a favorite aunt encamped behind the door. Appliances of this kind have enjoyed a nostalgic revival.

RIGHT ABOVE Italy has probably produced a greater variety of coffee-making equipment than any other country. Here a range of styles are displayed, joined by a sturdy juice extractor.

RIGHT BELOW Antique ceramic drawers for spices and dry goods are among the many details that suggest a traditional Italian kitchen.

Memories of times past crowd the kitchen and bathroom, but they introduce into the apartment a slightly disturbing touch of the surreal. Old-fashioned Italian terrazzo floors offer a nostalgia of their own.

ABOVE RIGHT A simple chair is set off to advantage by the tiled wall, which picks up a blurred shadow of its curved back rails.

RIGHT AND BELOW Speckled terrazzo continues into the bathroom floor and up the sides of the massive bathtub. The elaborate mirror frame was surely never meant to grace such a humble setting, but is both decorative and practical, and makes a good match for the traditional-style bathroom fixtures.

objects, reflecting the random and illogical aspects of life in a structured if always slightly unpredictable combination.

This spectacular apartment in Milan is full of objects that have been selected and arranged to stimulate the eye and the imagination as well as to serve the practical needs of everyday life. The church bench that half divides the dining area from the living room is an object which, if seen in its proper place, would not be at all remarkable. Here it not only causes a tremor of recognition— more potent, undoubtedly, for those of good Christian upbringing—but it reveals its strange and pleasing abstract shape, unlike any other piece of furniture from the normal domestic repertory. In its homey setting, it also provides three useful surfaces for putting things on as well as some additional seating. Here the white walls prevent the feeling from becoming too obsessive.

The hallway, with its typical Italian terrazzo floor sprinkled like the dusting of cocoa powder on a tiramisu, features a chair in richly painted folk-art baroque style and a wall cabinet whose lower doors sparkle with pieces of decorative colored glass like hard candy. The food and sweet-stuff metaphor continues with the picture made of beans and grains.

The oddest thing in the central room is the table pedestal. Perhaps its extended, tendrillike arm is meant to steady the precarious-looking marble top, but it gives it a disturbing sense of being alive. It has a couple of young, upwardly mobile relations in the two curly fruit bowls.

This is an apartment where the kitchen continues the decorative language of the other rooms, combining practicality with oddity in the presence of the old meat-slicing machine, the heavy weighing scales taken from an old corner shop, and a robust coffee grinder. The curtainless windows and the high white walls give a sense of freedom and release, while traditional storage jars and spice drawers promise good food to come. There is also a good central table, on well-turned legs, which looks like an unambiguous place for a traditional Italian family meal.

A taste for the unexpected or an unusual arrangement of objects keeps interest alive in every corner of the apartment as life flows by.

ABOVE Books, shoes, and suitcases have begun to proliferate. They create a miniature landscape on the floor, where the shoes inhabit striped bathing cabins and the suitcases evoke memories of faraway adventures.

OPPOSITE An elegant sleigh bed adds to the feeling of travel created by the artful disorder of the bedroom. At the same time, this is practical arrangement, where the old suitcases can provide additional storage space.

TASTE OF THE THIRTIES

The subdued and masculine air of this 1930s Antwerp apartment derives in part from the unusual quality of the original interiors—which were almost unaltered when the designer Eric De Queker bought it from its first owner. The apartment block itself is shaped to form an unusual pointed shiplike "prow," which gives the main living room four windows facing in different directions, overlooking a city park.

ABOVE One end of the Antwerp apartment building is shaped to resemble a ship's prow.

RIGHT Pieces of furry furniture stand on four legs. One has a tail, too.

FAR RIGHT The lay light in the hall ceiling establishes a strong geometry for the space, but the walls are attractively mobile as they curve to narrow the space at each end.

LEFT Simple colors
and rich textures combine
to create a luxurious feel
in this beautifully fitted-out
1930s apartment. The
original dado paneling,
incorporating radiator
cases, provides a strong
horizontal that is echoed
in lines of the furniture.

RIGHT The large leather
rug provides an exotic and
extravagant, but undeniably
comfortable, touch.

The use of traditional
materials—leather,
canvas, fur, and fine
wood veneers—evokes
the atmosphere of a
prewar liner or yacht.

Eric De Queker, who runs one of best-known furniture and interior design companies in Belgium, has created a subtle balance in his Antwerp apartment between the sense of nature outside and the feeling of warmth and enclosure within.

The fine veneered wood finishes of the doors, built-in cabinets, and wide archway that connects the two main parts of the living room set the tone for color and style, supported by the rich golden wood flooring.

The inner part of the living room—which was presumably originally intended to contain a substantial dining table—has a simple beamed ceiling, reminiscent of the early modernist villas of the Austrian architect Adolf Loos. Loos used such vestigial traditional details to differentiate spaces and give them character.

In this apartment the white-painted beams cast shadows and give perspective to the space. The inner area has been painted mushroom brown, while the view back from the far end of the room is framed by a bold gesture of black paint, setting the archway's wooden frame into relief. The bedroom, with wood paneling like that of a ship's cabin, is also painted to emphasize inward-looking comfort and contemplation, with a dark-blue ceiling suggestive of a night sky.

The view is framed by a bold gesture of black paint, setting the wooden frame of the archway into relief and creating a more mysterious feeling of "light beyond" in both directions.

Within this simple but luxurious framework, Eric De Queker has carefully placed individual items of furniture that match the apartment's color and mood. These include the low-slung wood and leather safari chairs, an inspiration for the modern furniture of Marcel Breuer and Le Corbusier in the 1920s, even though they were designed to be conveniently portable in a canvas bag rather than with any conscious intention of being "modern." The line of all the seating is equally low, and includes a long sofa by Nathalie van Reeth and gray-flannel-covered seating by Jean de Mulder. These unusual materials—the coffee table is covered in brown fur and stands

Flamboyant examples of modern lighting mean that the apartment gives the impression of a sharp contemporary mixture, rather than an interwar pastiche.

on a mat of black leather squares—reveal Eric De Queker's interest in texture as an aspect of design, something that usually works best, as here, within a limited color palette.

The broad hallway is veneered in striped rosewood and recalls the great ocean liners of the Art Deco period. Here the lighting, furniture, and picture hanging all bring attention down toward the floor, in preparation for the mood of the main rooms beyond. The bathroom is distinguished by its unusual double sink, a splendidly solid piece of interwar sanitaryware in an avocado color that matches the rest of the original fixtures. The fur rug takes the chill off the tiling and continues the tactile quality of the other rooms where it is most wanted.

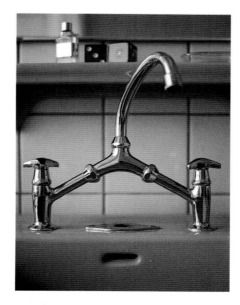

LEFT The two sets of faucets are each a miniature reflection of the larger unit.

RIGHT In a monumental bathroom such as this, the only sort of bathtub that seems appropriate is an old-fashioned rolltop.

INDOOR ROOF GARDEN

If you wander along the narrow streets of Milan, you may may be surprised by the sight of trees high up on the skyline. Growing on the upper terraces of apartment buildings, they form part of the most luxuriant roof gardens in Europe. In this elegant Milanese home, the trees and plants have been brought indoors as well, adding structure to the space as well as providing decoration.

THIS PICTURE Light falls invitingly onto the long sofa beneath the sloping roof. The fine Chinese pot containing the indoor tree is one of several decorative elements in a space that is otherwise white.

LEFT Trees and Eero Saarinen tables are grouped like families of objects. Behind the sofa is the dining area.

LEFT A room divider storing glass tableware divides the kitchen from the main space without loss of light. The overhead shelf is practical and decorative, as well as framing the opening to a more domestic scale and breaking up the light from beyond. Glass jars and other kitchen paraphernalia are stored on a ledge beneath the sloping roof.

BELOW LEFT The dining area is slightly darker than the rest of the apartment, allowing a greater sense of intimacy. Its rear wall is dissolved by reflections, while the delicate bubble of the antique glass chemist's jar on the table brings an element of the past into well-judged alignment with modern living.

G rowing plants indoors is now so popular and widespread a custom as perhaps to be unworthy of special mention, but the current trend in interior design goes against such a lively expression of nature inside the home, favoring a tight geometrical structure. It seems a shame to deny the potential of plants, however, for they have practical as well as decorative advantages for interiors, bringing freshness to the air and a general feeling of wellbeing.

The background of whiteness in paintwork and upholstery fabrics in this Milan apartment makes an excellent foil for the two big *Ficus benjamina* trees in the main living space. It is not difficult to imagine the different shadow patterns their leaves could cast by day or night. This simple color scheme is modified by well-chosen color accents, especially by the series of paperback books ranged in the deep shelves beneath the skylights. Other accents come from the blue glass jars on their high shelf, which seem to chime with the hydrangea blooms. The single touch of a pink carnation adds to this spectrum where aggressive color is absent.

LEFT A glimpse into the bathroom reveals a room that offers a generous sense of space in spite of its sloping ceiling. The towels are part of a series of blue objects whose careful placing helps to give a visual structure to the apartment.

In this apartment, objects are arranged in families—not only the trees and the books, but also the white Eero Saarinen tables. These 1960s furniture classics have re-emerged in the current revival of interest in the mid-20th-century period. There is no conflict, however, between these modernist tokens of high technology and the sofas and chairs, which belong to a refined version of the English country-house look. Details of an almost baroque richness pervade a more intimate sitting area, which has its own door onto the terrace.

One of the main unifying factors is light—coming from the side and above, it is bounced off the reflective wooden floor, nowhere interrupted by carpets or rugs, and off the mirrors. The large mirror leaning against the wall of the dining area and the overmantel mirror both stand close to glass doors that open onto the roof terraces, thus setting up two different kinds of reflection in the vertical plane, while the white table tops add their own milky lakes. White gloss finishes on the woodwork

Modern simplicity and the English country-house look are judiciously united in this Milan apartment by the clever use of light, white, and indoor trees.

RIGHT The large mirror propped up against the wall of the dining area has been deliberately placed near the window to maximize light and sense of space. The open door invites you to step out onto the greenery-filled roof terrace.

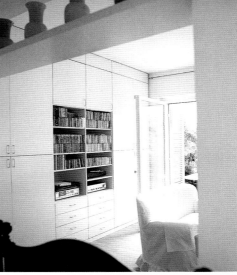

Trees indoors and out create a sense of enjoyable dislocation, where space ebbs and flows around simple pieces of furniture.

complete this effect of maximum light, but the matte textiles prevent it from becoming excessive and provide a pleasing contrast.

The realm of light that constitutes the dining room air is composed with subtle echoes of visual correspondence and rhythm—as seen in the curvaceous duet between the bureau's front and the serpentine lintel of the fireplace. The traditional open fireplace might come as a surprise in such an apartment, but its mannerist style, with its projecting shapes of white marble, suits the varied decorative language of the interior. Perhaps its aptness echoes the old alchemical division of the universe, for it adds fire to this microcosm of the elements of earth and air, amid pools of liquid light.

TRADITION WITH A TWIST

Lining the narrow cobbled streets of the Marais are some of Paris's oldest, most delightful houses. A swamp until it was reclaimed by monks in the 13th century, the area was adopted in the 17th century by high-society glitterati, who added fine mansions to the medieval architecture. When abandoned in favor of Faubourg St. Honoré and Faubourg St. Germain, the Marais fell into decline and became a slum, which it remained until regeneration in the 1960s. Today, the Marais again buzzes with life. Full of colorful shops, bars, cafés, restaurants, and galleries, it is a center for all lovers of art, history, and culture.

THIS PAGE AND OPPOSITE To avoid formality in the dining room, Gomez prefers to use mismatched china and napkins. The sleek, slimline table, made of dramatic wenge wood, is one of his designs for French furniture company Cinna. The charcoal drawings, found in a Parisian antiques shop, make a massive impact on the pale blue walls.

D idier Gomez is both a modernist and a classicist. Yes, his work is clearly contemporary—all sleek lines, subtle colors, and clever detailing—but there is something traditional, too, about its pleasing proportions and complete lack of look-at-me pretension. Born in Spain and now based in Paris, Gomez believes that the secret to his harmonious blend of old and new lies in his cross-cultural upbringing: a combination of the passion and drama of the Spanish and the effortless chic of the French. Chief furniture designer for Ligne Roset, he also designed the Carousel du Louvre shopping complex and offices for Louis Vuitton, Christian Dior, Kenzo, Chanel, and Cartier.

Gomez's home is a spacious apartment in the Marais district of Paris. Once a lovely 19th-century townhouse, the building was being used as a pharmaceutical factory when he first saw it. It was dark, full of machinery, and, worst of all, the garden had been covered over and turned into a production line. Fortunately, the wonderful proportions of the rooms remained.

After all the factory clutter had been removed, little was done to alter the building's structure, but Gomez increased the height of doorways, laid parquet floors—wenge in the bedroom, bleached oak everywhere else—and, most importantly, restored the garden to its original glory, planting mature trees and hedges in a formal scheme.

The apartment folds itself around the garden in a U-shape, so it is key to the way he lives: the views create a sense of country-in-the-city; he

"In my job I am always working with different materials and colors, so at home I need somewhere very quiet and serene, outside the noise of the city," says designer Didier Gomez.

loves the sound of birdsong and the serenity of having green space in the center of Paris.

There is a deceptive subtlety about this apartment. At first, it appears very French: calm and quiet, decorated in cool colors and clean lines. But then you notice the intriguing touches that hint at Gomez's Spanish blood and his love of combining disparate elements: a vivid red throw over the arm of the sofa, a 1930s African artwork made of leather, an Eames chair from the 1940s, an imposing quartet of 1936 charcoal drawings, a pair of early 20th-century armchairs by the French decorator André Arbus.

Gomez, one suspects, is easily bored and enjoys the variety of a mix-and-match approach. He is careful not to overdo it, though—his skill lies in knowing just when to stop. He uses ethnic artefacts, for example, but you couldn't describe this apartment as "ethnic"; he uses 20th-century classics, but it is far from being "retro." Neither Spanish nor French, old nor new, it is what it is: the epitome of one man's inimitable vision.

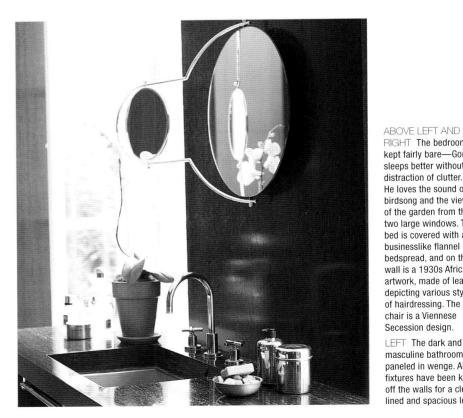

ABOVE LEFT AND RIGHT The bedroom is kept fairly bare—Gomez sleeps better without the distraction of clutter. He loves the sound of birdsong and the views of the garden from the two large windows. The bed is covered with a businesslike flannel bedspread, and on the wall is a 1930s African artwork, made of leather, depicting various styles of hairdressing. The chair is a Viennese Secession design.

LEFT The dark and masculine bathroom is paneled in wenge. All the fixtures have been kept off the walls for a clean-lined and spacious look.

A combination of the passion and drama of the Spanish and the effortless chic of the French lies at the heart of this harmonious blend of old and new.

THIS PAGE AND INSET PICTURES The floor and tub are made of concrete. Their pale color sets up a strong contrast with the dark wenge all around. A toilet and shower are hidden in the cupboards. The fixtures are from the Conran Shop in Paris. Though modern, they are reminiscent of classical shapes—a touch that is typical of Gomez. Waffle towels, a row of votives and a pair of pretty matte-metal lidded pots soften the otherwise minimal look of the room in an unobtrusive way.

HARLEM HERITAGE

Founded by Dutch farmers as Dutch Nieuw Haarlem in 1658, the uptown district of Harlem was a bucolic retreat for almost three centuries. Not until the area was linked to lower Manhattan by rail did it see much in the way of residential development. In the early 19th century, the fabulously rich fur trader and merchant John Jacob Astor built his family a country home and stables in rural Harlem. Bridle paths cleared for the Astor horses were the antecedents of the long, looping drives that thread their way through the rustic north end of Central Park.

arlem became in the early years of the 20th century the focus of a "City Beautiful" movement, attracting a newly prosperous Jewish population eager to escape the tenements of the Lower East Side. In 1901, one of Manhattan's earliest apartment buildings, Graham Court, was erected just a few blocks north of the park. Catering to a Jewish clientele, the eight-story-high, block-wide edifice, designed by Clinton & Russell, featured a large central courtyard, multiple entrances, generous high-ceilinged apartments—and kitchens with the two sinks necessary for preparing kosher foods. Lighting fixtures and porcelain wood-look logs in the fireplaces were fueled by gas.

Soon after, New York's real estate market went bust. Bucking the trend, an enterprising realtor of African-American heritage, Philip Payton, bought up leases throughout Harlem and, in turn, offered reasonable rents to the hundreds of African-American families who had been dislocated by development farther downtown. By the heyday of the so-called Harlem Renaissance of the 1920s,

OPPOSITE The Egyptian Pink dining-room walls provide the perfect foil for the mahogany wainscoting, and for the mantel that Warner Johnson himself stripped and restored. He maintains its sheen with a special polish called Dughe, made in Paris, whose scent he particularly likes.

ABOVE The door to the dining room is the only one in the apartment that has been taken back to its original mahogany. Johnson and Cabot found the elegant dining table in an antique store on New York's Bond Street; the chairs are French.

RIGHT The oculus mirror was cracked when Johnson bought it; he left it as it was.

over 50,000 blacks lived in the area; Graham Court was a premiere address for the black intelligentsia. Unfortunately, America's Great Depression brought about another reversal of fortune, one that the neighborhood struggled for decades—with little success—to combat. Race riots and rampant vandalism added to the agony. By the late 1970s, Graham Court had run down to such an extent that there was no running water and heat was virtually non-existent.

With the prosperity of the 1980s, though, the neighborhood began, once again, to turn around. Graham Court's noble beauty was recognized by enterprising young African-American professionals, among them Warner Johnson, a telecommunication entrepreneur who had received his master's degree in business from nearby Columbia University. Johnson joined a community of like-minded individuals who were committed to protecting the dowager apartment building from the "progressive" overhaul that was desecrating other commercial and residential buildings in the city. Today, the building stands just outside—but nonetheless anchors—one corner of an historic district that includes Mount Morris Park, one of the last remnants of the area's arcadian past. Thus, when the opportunity arose, Johnson snapped up a classic, 3,200 square foot (300 square meter), nine-room rental on one of Graham Court's upper stories.

Having lived in Paris after graduate school, as well as in New York City's Greenwich Village, Johnson came to his new apartment with a mélange of furnishings, artworks, and items, such as Moroccan rugs and a matador's jacket, he had picked up on his travels abroad. He then invited a friend of eight years, designer Edward Cabot, to help him organize the miscellany—and give the apartment a feeling of coherence.

Cabot's main thrust in his "re-adjustment"of the apartment was to create a dramatic backdrop for Johnson's possessions by painting each room a shimmering, fully saturated hue. Once the two men had decided on the tone for every room, Cabot had the paint mixed and made in England.

THIS PAGE Originally
a bedroom, the vibrant
yellow room across the
hall from the billiards
room now serves as
Johnson's library. The
seagrass rug in front of
the fireplace is accented
with a Moroccan rug
from Marrakesh.

OPPOSITE The living
room is painted a dark,
moody olive. The
Oriental-style rug was
bought on 125th Street
for a mere $8.

LEFT Sand-peach walls temper the effects of the sunlight filtering through the matchstick blinds in one of the two guest bedrooms. The room is a study in how Johnson acquired his furnishings. In the early days of his collecting, he could afford only very cheap items, such as the stripped pine table. Even when adding more expensive pieces, as he does from time to time, he always looks for a quirky, idiosyncratic quality that sets them off as originals.

Walls are painted rich and evocative hues to set off personal collections, and every object in the apartment is redolent of a "misunderstood past."

"I could get the dimensionality I wanted there," he says, noting how he "forcefully" persuaded Johnson to "carry back the paint cans" on various overseas flights. Thus, the billiard room, for example, wears the lustrous, midnight-blue color of coal freshly scooped from the scuttle, while the library is a tangy sunshine yellow.

The apartment's "bones" were surprisingly sound. After almost a century of wear, though, the chestnut floors had to be refinished, and the fireplaces required a thorough refurbishing, even though their gas logs had been disconnected years before. Johnson's furnishings had to be augmented, so Cabot led him on many forays in the city and up the Hudson River to add pieces the two felt were missing from each room. Cabot calls their finds "dispossessed objects" that evoke what he calls a "misunderstood past." Johnson wanted his rooms to embody a nuanced, impressionistic sense of that past. That he and Cabot achieved this is a gift to the apartment, and to this most historic address.

RIGHT The plain pine table beside the bed sometimes serves as a simple desk.

OPPOSITE The master bed is draped in a French Provençal bedspread banded in bold hues. Among "dispossessed objects" found on trips abroad are a matador's jacket from Spain and a Moroccan fez. These are suspended from one of the sconces original to the building, which had been pulled from the walls and left abandoned in the basement. The chestnut flooring found throughout is a rarity in apartments.

STREAMLINED SLEEK

A legacy of the 20th century is the conversion of vast former workspaces into habitable lofts. Often located in gritty industrial areas, these vast floor-throughs lured artists who could not afford to buy or rent somewhere large enough in which to produce their work. Urban pioneers all, they turned the raw spaces into studios where they could both live and create, sometimes making do without basic utilities, and paying little or no rent. In time, other entrepreneurs caught the fever, so that today swathes of former warehouse buildings have become so gentrified that the artists have had to move on. Lofts in neighborhoods such as Manhattan's SoHo and London's Clerkenwell command prices or rents that surpass those for places of equal size in more respectable areas. The typical urban loft is bright and airy, with large expanses of glass. Sparsely adorned, it may incorporate unexpected features—a rooftop reflecting pool, for example, a beaded curtain, or a wall of rough-sawn wood. This is minimalism with a message: home is a gallery for living.

LEFT Separating the store from the dining area and kitchen is a pond full of koi carp, surrounded by a frequently changing collection of plants. The huge skylight, which fills the room with light, was already in place when Riss bought the property, although it had to be renovated.

RIGHT Riss and her two children each have a floor above the store, joined by an industrial metal staircase. Large sliding doors make a bold statement at the entrance to their apartments.

THE WHITEST SHADE OF PALE

This Brussels house brings a new meaning to the notion of living over the store. It belongs to a Belgian fashion designer whose work and private lives are so closely interwoven that it is impossible to tell where one starts and the other stops. The backdrop to both lives is an utterly simple design concept that creates a hugely powerful look: the color white is used almost uniformly everywhere, from walls and floors to furnishings and textiles. Disciplined yet gentle, pure yet comfortable, plain yet sophisticated, the result is a peaceful space that provides an arena for boundless creativity.

White, in the West, is often associated with purity and chastity. In Asia it is worn for mourning, and in Africa it is regarded as a protection against evil spirits. There is no disputing the universal power of white—at once a non-color (made up of all the other colors in the spectrum) and the most potent color of all. To layer white with white in a home is both very simple and very brave.

"I have always dreamed of having a pure white house," says Johanne Riss. "In fact, I can only live in white—it's what enables me to create." Riss's home, in the modern quarter of Brussels, is a pure example of white-on-white living—an airy, dreamlike space with a soft, feminine charm, just like her timeless clothes designs.

It wasn't always like this. Once a storage depot for bananas, the building was a restaurant when Riss bought it in 1990. She renovated the central glass skylight that allows light to flood in through the ground floor, but took out everything else to start again. "I wanted pure, clean lines,

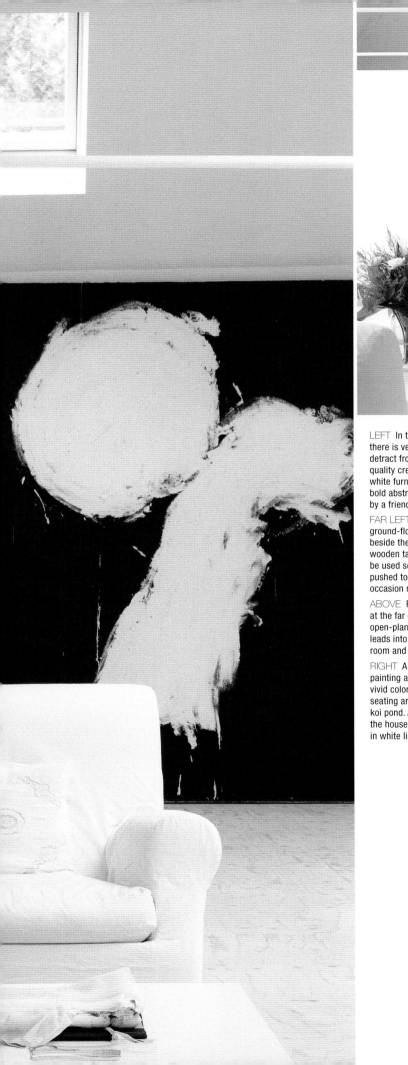

LEFT In the living space there is very little to detract from the ethereal quality created by the all-white furnishings. The bold abstract painting is by a friend of the owner.

FAR LEFT In the ground-floor dining area beside the pond, small wooden tables can be used separately or pushed together as the occasion requires.

ABOVE Riss's bed is at the far end of her open-plan loft, which leads into her dressing room and bathroom.

RIGHT A dramatic painting adds a touch of vivid color to another seating area near the koi pond. All the chairs in the house are covered in white linen or cotton.

In every space, a feeling of calm and tranquility predominates, thanks to the disciplined use of clean, pared-down lines and a limited color palette.

with nothing unnecessary added," she explains. Johanne Riss's first priority was the basement, which became the atelier where her couture clothes are made, and the ground floor—shared between her store and the private kitchen and dining area where she eats with her son and daughter, and also entertains. The store includes evening wear, cocktail dresses, and Riss's trademark wedding dresses, hung in an all-white space surrounded by raw metal. Between the two spaces is a large pond filled with Japanese koi carp, which swim among waterlilies, bathed in light from the skylight above. Around the pond are plants in both tubs and small indoor beds— the plants are changed every six months or so.

It took seven years for Johanne Riss to finish the rest of the building, but eventually the three upper floors were converted into loftlike living and

ABOVE LEFT AND RIGHT Riss sometimes changes the way her bed is dressed, but it is always simple and romantic, covered with white linen and framed by sheer hangings.

LEFT AND OPPOSITE The ornately carved and painted four-poster bed was brought back from a trip to India. It now stands in Riss's daughter's bedroom, where its dark wood provides an exciting contrast to the white furnishings elsewhere.

bedroom spaces for her and her children. Linking one floor with another are open-tread metal staircases, bold and industrial in style—and highly practical. Huge, floor-to-ceiling sliding doors made from wood and glass lead into the children's lofts, while Riss's own spacious, open-plan apartment features a wooden library door.

Not only are walls and floors uniformly white, but sofas, chairs, and cushions are all covered in white linen or cotton; the coffee table is white, the bed coverings and even the bookcases are white. The exception is the art: large, exuberant abstract paintings, sometimes in bold colors, all by Riss's friends, add a dramatic counterpoint to the otherwise monochrome scheme.

Even the bathroom adheres to a strict purity of style. The white-painted brick walls and floors provide a neutral backdrop for a large square bathtub. A wall-mounted faucet, by Vola, is sleek and minimal, and an entire wall of unobtrusive storage keeps clutter out of sight. Piles of neatly folded towels are stacked on simple shelving. Just like the rest of the house, this is a haven for relaxation, where the subtle, purifying, and healing powers of an all-white space banish any suggestion of stress or disturbance.

THIS PAGE AND OPPOSITE At first glance, the bathroom may seem ascetic, but it is designed for maximum comfort and relaxation. The lack of color makes it incredibly tranquil, while capacious storage means that there is no clutter to distract or disturb. The fixtures are minimal, but well sized, brilliantly functional, and very chic. And what saves the room from bland uniformity is the range of intriguing textures, from the glossy painted brickwork to the fluffy towels, the slightly distressed wooden floor, and the smooth, cool, rectangular bathtub.

URBAN RETREAT

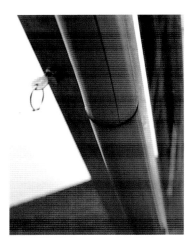

In the center of gridlocked, overcrowded London, it is almost impossible to find a site on which to build—but one young architect did just that, and in the process created a house that reflects all the finesse of the city but feels as if it were miles away from the stresses of urban life. Simple, but not plain, it is spacious, full of light, and imbued with a sense of calm and quiet.

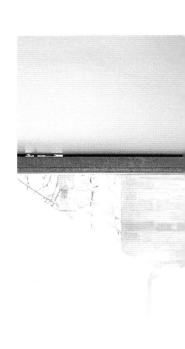

LEFT While the rest of the house is neutral, the hallway has a dash of bold color. Seagrass matting dyed dramatic crimson and a ceiling to match frame the entrance. Lined with floor-to-ceiling storage, the walls have hidden push-hinge openings.

ABOVE LEFT The entrance door is made of steel-framed glass with a bamboo pull.

RIGHT The huge glass doors allow a view through to the internal courtyard, which features a trough planted with bamboo and a wet wall. The concrete floor in the living area stretches right outside, emphasizing the sense of space. Ian Chee himself designed the traditional Japanese paper lamp and the railroad-tie daybed.

LEFT The sophisticated kitchen incorporates a combination of lacquered wood, glass, and glossy black laminate. The storage area is hidden by translucent doors made of inexpensive expanded polycarbonate. A frosted-glass overhang forms the breakfast bar. Classic Oxford dining chairs by Arne Jacobsen are paired with a 1950s Heal's table.

ABOVE Light pours into the dining area through an overhead skylight. The painting—of grass—is by Andy Harper.

OPPOSITE, LEFT AND RIGHT The dining area is illuminated by inset floor lights and sculptural, directional wall lamps.

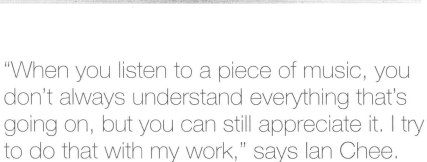

"When you listen to a piece of music, you don't always understand everything that's going on, but you can still appreciate it. I try to do that with my work," says Ian Chee.

While some contemporary architecture is deliberately ostentatious, screaming, "Look at me! Look at me!," other buildings are more demure, modestly revealing their secrets only after a interval of respectful contemplation. This house, in a quiet cul-de-sac in West London, is most definitely one of the latter.

Known as the T-house (the plan is in the shape of a T), it was built by architect Ian Chee on the site of a former taxi garage—a location that was found only after many months of intensive searching that involved real estate agents, auctions, and the internet. It was Chee's first new-build project, which gave him an opportunity to design every last detail from scratch.

A height restriction inspired Chee to devise a curving roof—which, far from being a limitation, adds a cozy, secure feel to the upstairs rooms. On the ground floor, the architect created an L-shaped living space encompassing a kitchen, living room, and dining area.

The most immediately striking feature of the living space is a huge wall of glass that gives views of an internal garden. The installation of a skylight over the dining table allowed light to flood in, despite the lack of conventional windows. The floor—made of poured concrete polished to a softly textured sheen—continues through to the courtyard, so that the exterior is a genuine extension of what's inside.

This sense of flowing from space to space is as important to this house as its structural components. Chee was a musician before he became an architect, and he acknowledges the similarities between the two endeavors: "Many things work on a subliminal level. When you listen to a piece of music, you don't always understand everything that's going on, but you can still appreciate it. I try to do that with my work."

Subliminal, subtle, sophisticated—all describe Ian Chee's home equally well. "I like living in a very simple way," he says. "You try to let your personality come out rather than the space overwhelm you. It should form an interesting backdrop that you can play off."

ABOVE Airy and spacious, the living area is restful, calm, and quiet. Light from the glass doors is reflected on the concrete floor, which has been gently polished to reveal the color and texture of the aggregate. The white sofa is by Italian designer Antonio Citterio, with cushions that Chee covered in Chinese silk brocade. The coffee table is a 1950s Danish piece. A wastepaper basket from Muji was used to make the plant stand.

LEFT Chee bought the teak folding stool on a roadside in Bali.

LEFT AND FAR LEFT
The metal staircase with glass treads is almost a reverse of a normal staircase. Suspended above a corner of the living room, it resembles a modern sculpture.

BELOW Nothing has been allowed to interfere with the clear, simple lines of this large room. Smooth walls (with a shadow gap at the base rather than a baseboard) complement the concrete floor. Underfloor heating avoids the clutter of radiators. Even the furniture is raised on legs, creating a sense that is it is floating.

LEFT An oversized frosted window adds drama to the sleek bathroom, where Chee has combined a range of intriguing materials and textures. The floor is made of unglazed ceramic tiles and the walls of waterproof render. The basin is boxed in with stainless-steel panelling and the walk-in shower-bath is paneled with a sheet of clear glass.

RIGHT A monumental granite curbstone forms a step into the bedroom. Again, simplicity is key. Chee designed the bed with a metal frame and wooden paneling that forms the integral headrest and side table.

Underfloor heating, hidden storage, and a lack of moldings, baseboards, and other unnecessary frills means that visual disturbance is avoided and every detail really counts.

Despite its apparent simplicity, the house yields a few thoughtful surprises. The downstairs living space, with its clean lines and uncluttered openness, is punctuated by a series of unusual design elements: the kitchen island, made of glass; a large skylight, which illuminates the dining area; a narrow trough in the floor, in which grows a bamboo screen; and an amazing metal-and-glass staircase, which is suspended in a corner of the living area like a piece of modern sculpture. Elsewhere, neutrality prevails, in the shape of smooth plaster walls, pared-down, square-shaped furniture, and cool colors, with a hide rug, brocade cushions, and an abstract painting adding textural contrasts.

Upstairs, the house becomes more intimate. A window in the bathroom (frosted for privacy) opens onto the terrace, and a wall of mirrors, with storage behind, increases the sense of space. All the fixtures are suspended above the floor, and a glass panel forms the side of the walk-in shower-bath, creating a feel of floating and lightness. The corridor is lined with full-length storage flush to the walls, with concealed openings, so that all evidence of day-to-day paraphernalia can be hidden away. And in the bedroom, too, nothing disturbs the deep sense of calm. Just minutes from the cacophony of shops, traffic, and commerce, this is a haven of quiet, a gentle sonata composed with grace and harmony in mind.

MEXICAN HOTHOUSE

While offering a totally modern response to the demands of the unrelenting sun and the rigors of urban living, this house on the western edge of Mexico City has ancient architectural roots that give it a timeless feel. Its style was partly inspired by Islamic and Mediterranean forms of architecture.

Despite the bold colors of this dramatic retreat in Las Lomas, in the hills on the western edge of Mexico City, and the occasional glimpses it offers of trees and ravines, this is a house that turns in on itself and the earth. If the architect who designed it were to be asked who or what was the source of its inspiration, his answer would be: the great Mexican architect Luis Barragán. When, in 1980, Barragán won architecture's equivalent of the Nobel Prize, he stated his ideal for modern architecture. Buildings were, he said, to have a sense of serenity, mystery, silence, privacy, and the power to astonish. For good measure, he also added sorcery and enchantment.

When its architect-owner demolished an earlier house that stood on this site in order to build a new one, he followed Barragán's principles to the letter. The result is a place truly imbued with serenity, mystery, and enchantment. As you approach it from the outside world and walk through its rooms and spaces, some of them carved out of the earth and clinging on below ground level, you are filled with a sense of gradual revelation. It is as though the house were reluctant to reveal its true nature except to the few permitted to enter its innermost, most intimate recesses. It is a building that Barragán would surely have described as "an architectural striptease."

The "striptease" starts as soon as you see the house. Surrounded by high, protective walls, it is completely cut off and self-contained, though a hint of trees, barely glimpsed over the walls, gives

THIS PAGE AND OPPOSITE The house was constructed using traditional red-clay bricks covered in a cement-and-gravel render and painted over with specially mixed paints. The colors really come into their own in the courtyard, which plays a central role in the life of the house. Here each plane of the pink-toned walls shades from yellow to orange, to peach, to tangerine, as the sun moves around through the day. The courtyard is stepped like a pre-Columbian temple, with its steps planted with *magueyes* or tropical agaves. The steps conceal a garage.

THIS PAGE AND
OPPOSITE, INSET
Above the staircase
leading down to the main
living area, a skylight
has been covered with
a yellow concrete lattice,
which mirrors the design
of the ventilation holes
in a side wall. The light
that comes through
throws ever-changing
patterns on the walls.

OPPOSITE, MAIN
PICTURE A corridor-
staircase leads down to
the master bedroom and
bathroom. Here, a ceiling
constructed from spaced
concrete tubes allows
light to enter and play
on the walls.

a tempting illusion of countryside. Intensifying the sense of isolation, two steep ravines, one on each side of the house, form an unbreachable barrier between the family who lives here and the urban cacophony that carries on unceasingly outside the walls.

Once you have penetrated the enormous rusted-steel door, a narrow, high-sided corridor leads you to the stepped inner courtyard whose proportions are a humbling reminder of the insignificance of human life. From here, another massive door, this time made of stone, opens onto a curved upper reception area, cleverly lit by an opening let into the top of the wall. Its many curves give the building a calming, human touch.

From the reception area, a descending staircase, lit by a concrete lattice skylight, leads to a service area and offices, then a second

staircase takes you on down deeper into the earth to a vestibule, and to the living areas— sitting, dining, library (the most heavily used part of the house), bedrooms, and bathrooms. At this level, many of the rooms surrounding the inner courtyard open onto it, their large glass windows sliding back for ease of access.

Although the house is determinedly minimalist in both design and concept, it could never be described as lacking a heart. Its owner-architect has devised a place to live that is devoid of excess—not to depersonalize it, but to provide himself and his family with space to relax and breathe. It gives them what many of us have all too little of: "time to stand and stare." No doubt Luis Barragán would approve.

ABOVE LEFT AND LEFT The owner plays subtle games with light and color, repeating exterior colors on interior walls. In this vibrantly colored dining area, dominated by an oversized still life of yellow fruit, even the watermelons contribute to the fiery theme. The bleached wooden chairs and sideboard, the bright white bowls and jars, and the ultra-pale floor covering bring down the temperature in what would otherwise be an unbearably hot zone.

LEFT AND RIGHT The courtyard is paved with local volcanic pebbles, while massive early bronze pots point the way to the stone door that leads into the house.

ABOVE RIGHT A monolithic dark stone door leads into the curved upper hallway paved with a white stone relief-patterned floor. Light floods in through an opening where wall and ceiling meet.

For Luis Barragán, the architect who inspired this house, the ideal building should bring together serenity, mystery, silence, and privacy with the power to astonish—spiced up with elements of sorcery and enchantment.

Although the house is determinedly minimalist in both design and concept, it could never be described as lacking a heart.

ABOVE Many of the rooms surrounding the inner courtyard open onto it. Squares of local volcanic stone on the terrace are divided by bands of white marble, an effect that is mirrored by the large windows. One section of the terrace consists of a raised triangular slab of black marble.

RIGHT In the master bedroom, a yellow wall and sofa sing out against the neutral colors and natural wood tones.

ABOVE LEFT AND LEFT In the bathroom, circular monumental stone shapes and the color yellow pick up themes that have been used elsewhere in the house. The shaving mirror has been strategically placed to reflect the huge Matisse print hanging on the wall.

ROOM WITH A VIEW

This small open-plan apartment combines a powerful architectural aesthetic with all the advantages of a bustling inner-city location. It forms part of a low-rise 1950s complex— built to house local workers such as nurses and police officers, and now protected from unsuitable development. A full-width arched window creates a wall of glass, flooding the space with light and outlining panoramic views of east London. Several ingenious alterations have successfully revitalized the space by acknowledging the spirit and integrity of the original concept without creating a set piece of design history.

THIS PAGE AND OPPOSITE The apartment is a compact rectangular shape, with a wall of glass situated in front of the relaxing zone. The view from the entrance shows the kitchen area to the left, the sitting area directly ahead, and the sleeping area in a open box to the right. Arched windows at the back and front of the space are linked by a barrel-shaped ceiling.

LEFT A few minor but effective adjustments transformed this open-plan area into a compact and convenient inner-city base. Such updating is not always successful. The powerful aesthetics of 1950s, 1960s, and 1970s architecture can dominate a scheme and get in the way of a simple rationalization of the space.

FAR RIGHT AND RIGHT Simple white window shades modulate and diffuse incoming light, changing the emphasis from the internal to the external environment.

BELOW Dividing the kitchen and the main living area is the original storage system, with a combination of open and solid-back shelving.

This London apartment—one of a series of open-plan units designed for single or double occupancy—is located on the top floor of a low-rise inner-city building. The building is part of Golden Lane Estate, a 1950s government-housing complex built for local blue-collar professionals by architects Chamberlin, Powell & Bon—who also designed the adjacent Barbican Estate (see pages 148–55 and 156–61).

Acknowledging and understanding the history of the apartment is an important part of the responsibility shouldered by its owner, but also adds to the excitement of living here—even though regulations and restrictions sometimes protect the wrong thing, such as an unauthentic replacement kitchen. While the owner's ambition is restoration, even returning the kitchen to something like its original simplicity now requires what is called listed building consent.

The apartment's full-width arched window and barrel-shaped ceiling are exclusive to the top-floor units in the building and contribute to the

high levels of light and general sense of space. A wall of glass on one side frames a panorama of east London. The overall impression of luminosity and space have a memorable impact on anyone entering the apartment; they draw the eye past the kitchen area set to one side of the entrance and into the main living area beyond.

Seventy percent of the space is occupied by a living area whose various seating configurations define different activities. For example, there are chairs arranged around a table for eating or working, chairs positioned for contemplating the view from the window, and a group configuration including a sofa that invites conversation and socializing. A solitary lounger, reading light, and occasional table, together with a large collection of design and photographic books, signal the key area of interest and activity.

The simple storage system for books is one of the new additions to the space. Running the full length of the living area, the shelving provides an opportunity for both storage and display.

In full view from the lounger, the sleeping zone is an open box one step up from the main living area. The change in level, a wall panel intersecting the storage unit, and the chain-link curtain are all new additions. The wall and the chain divider provide an ingenious division between areas without compromising ease of transition or the impression of overall openness. They underline what is remarkable about this compact space. Different areas interconnect in a logical sequence, but also manage to convey a sense of independence and change in style specific to their different functions.

Different areas of the apartment interconnect in a logical sequence, but at the same time manage to convey a sense of independence and change in style that is specific to their separate functions.

ABOVE AND LEFT
Attention to detail on the part of the original architects means that there are several useful open storage solutions built into the kitchen and relaxing areas—vital in a space of this kind. Chairs are positioned to define different activities. For example, the key area of interest is dominated by a solitary lounger.

LEFT Hanging a chain-link curtain across the opening between the main sitting area and sleeping zone provides an inventive screen.

FAR LEFT ABOVE A shelving tower provides storage for shirts and can be spun around to face the wall, leaving a single shelf on view for beside items.

FAR LEFT BELOW Open storage for books, with sliding aluminum panels to break up the display, continues right into the sleeping areas.

ABOVE AND LEFT Raw bricks and stained wooden panels have been teamed with contemporary chrome fixtures to offset white tiling with a warm, natural material.

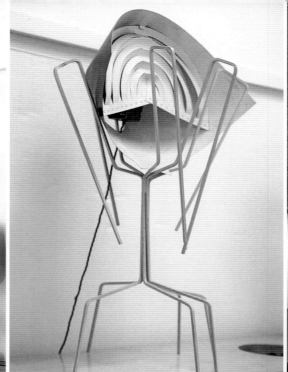

LEFT Dark wood is used in the drawing room in the form of slatted-front storage cabinets, a radiator cover that doubles as a bench, and adjustable louvered shutters. The floor is covered with unobtrusive woven-paper matting. The 1940s leather chair is by Finn Juhl.

ABOVE, LEFT TO RIGHT Slim battens line the walls so that art can be arranged and rearranged as desired. The painting is by the owner's son Zebedee. On the slatted shelf are an ancient South Sea Island neckrest and a goblet by French designer and sculptor Paul Jouve. The constructivist lamp is by Ben Jones, another son of the owner. An abstract sculpture in ebony by Alexander Noll sits next to the wooden handle of a ceremonial adze.

AT HOME WITH ART

In the London home of an interior designer, each individual element works hard for its keep. But practicality is combined with artistic expression, for this is a house which contains an impressive collection of eclectic pieces, ranging from classic 20th-century designer chairs to antique ethnic artefacts. The displays are constantly evolving and altering, but the ethos remains the same: to please, surprise, and stimulate.

LEFT An extraordinary 1930s chair, one of a pair, is covered in python skin. Wall-mounted adjustable lamps, subtle and versatile, are used throughout the house.

RIGHT The leather side chairs are by Chester Jones. Behind them sit, from left to right, a Chinese lacquered bean case, a Japanese woven basket, a ceremonial adze handle, a vicious-looking 16th-century wooden gaming glove, and an elegant 1940s lamp by Alvar Aalto. Jones is enthralled by the juxtaposition of objects: "The whole is greater than the sum of the parts," he says.

BELOW The Japanese basket adds textural contrast when set against shiny wood and smooth leather.

The owner's fascination with the strangeness of objects, combined with a love of 20th-century furniture and art, lies at the root of his collecting.

Chester Jones doesn't believe in comfort—or too much comfort, at any rate. The architect and interior designer reckons that anyone can make a place comfortable. "As long as you have a modicum of comfort, it's better to have something challenging," he says. But his house in central London does not appear to be lacking in comfort; nor does it challenge in an obvious or difficult way. Rather, it reveals itself gradually as being full of surprises, of precious treasures and intriguing pieces. He designed the house as an empty space, but found that "it just attracted objects" and now, four years later, it is full of them; indeed, it has the air of a gallery in its careful displays and calm atmosphere.

ABOVE In a corner of the dining room, the unusual reverse cutout lamp is a modern piece made of bronze.

LEFT The pantry is lined with simple tongue-and-groove paneling, painted white. On open shelves blue and white dishes are piled up to make an unassuming display.

RIGHT Typically French, the 1930s pressed-steel café chairs add a bright splash of color to the dining room. The picture on the wall is by Chester Jones's son Ben, as is the nearby lamp.

OPPOSITE, RIGHT "The dining room is full of colorful bits of nonsense," says Jones.

This was once a traditionally decorated family home, informal and mismatched, on three floors with a basement below. But after the Joneses' children had grown up and left, it was time for a total overhaul, not just of soft furnishings and paint colors, but of the ways and means by which an extensive range of art and artefacts could be both stored and set out. A copious amount of storage was the key, taking the form of large, built-in cupboards in every room. Chester Jones loathes conventional cupboards, so he designed units with slatted doors that both conceal and teasingly reveal their contents, with none of the blank heaviness of solid doors. In the drawing room they are made from iroko, stained the same color as the polished teak floors, and perfectly complementing the slatted wooden radiator covers and louvered window shutters.

All this dark wood delineates the space in a dramatic, graphic way, fusing form and function. The same goes for the walls, which have a series of battens for hanging pictures. As in a gallery, the display of objects changes on a regular basis. Jones feels impelled to change things that have become overfamiliar, and this arrangement allows

LEFT The bathroom, paneled with French-polished iroko, is as dark and enveloping as the drawing room. The basin, bathtub, and countertops are made of black marble, and the sculptural faucet is by Philippe Starck. The round mirror is a classic design by Eileen Gray.

RIGHT The bed stands on a rug designed by Sandy Jones. While dark wood dominates the room, simple anthracite-colored linen curtains hang at the windows, and the clothes closets are made from raffia panels stretched over slim iroko frames. The bedside lamp is a 1930s example by Boris-Jean Lacroix.

INSET RIGHT Above the bookcase hangs an abstract realist painting by Kate Nicholson, the daughter of Ben Nicholson.

BELOW The folding wood and cane chair, designed in 1949, is by Hans Wegner.

for an almost infinite variety of hangings. "I think houses and interiors are much more about living in the mind than living in reality," he says. "It's about feeding the curiosity, the ability to be excited, to grow into a place and to extend yourself. I always try to find solutions that aren't stereotyped and tired. When you decorate, it must be a one-off, using strange, peculiar things that you half recognize but that are elusive."

He is particularly fascinated by things that contain an element of surprise, whether it be a skeletal constructivist lamp, a chair covered in python skin or a giant Chinese bean case. The curious, dynamic juxtapositions that result are what pleases Jones and his designer wife, Sandy—for a few months, at least, until the urge to change it all around overcomes them again.

"It's either this or minimalism," says Jones. "When you live in a city, you need a place in which to withdraw and be quiet, where the pace of life can slow down. You can either have a white box with nothing in it, or you can fill your home with objects that you can handle and contemplate." White box this definitely is not, but as a place for stimulation, contemplation, and relaxation, it wins hands down every time.

HOLLYWOOD NATURAL

The 1950s ushered in a golden era of sophisticated, relaxed houses in which the potential of lightweight steel frames and glass walls, reflecting pools, and remarkable sites was explored in original and powerful ways. The architecture was matched by the seductive black and white images of the great architectural photographer Julius Schulman. In 1959, the architect Richard Neutra designed such a house for a Los Angeles couple, Mr. and Mrs. Henry Lew, on a dramatic sloping site on Sunset Plaza Drive.

FAR LEFT The two-story house is entered from the upper floor at street level. Steps at the rear lead down to a sloping garden.

THIS PICTURE At the rear of the house, an external balcony and deck run alongside the long glazed volume of the living room. Sliding glass doors separate the deck from the interior, so that in warm weather it becomes an extension of the living area.

Mies van der Rohe at work

ABOVE Sliding glass doors extend the living space onto the deck, allowing owners and guests to make the most of California's equable climate.

RIGHT Architects such as Frank Lloyd Wright made the hearth the nucleus of the home. If there is a comparable sacred spot in a Richard Neutra house, it is the deck or terrace.

In a Neutra house, the inspirational use of glass means that the relationship between indoors and outside space is charged with ambiguity.

An Austrian émigré who settled in the USA in the early 1920s, the architect Richard Neutra saw huge opportunities to exploit lightweight materials such as steel and glass to create flexible spaces and structures. As the American critic Barbara Lamprecht records in *Richard Neutra—Complete Works*, published in 2000, over decades Neutra developed and refined a "family" of details, including metal and aluminum casement windows.

One of Neutra's earliest projects was the Lovell Health House in Los Angeles, completed in 1929. Designed for Philip and Leah Lovell, a wealthy couple who promoted active, healthy lifestyles, it was the first light steel-framed house in the USA. It is also a house that addresses the art of living in Los Angeles, a city of wide flat valleys interrupted by canyons and hills.

The two-story house Neutra designed in 1959 for Mr. and Mrs. Henry Lew on Sunset Plaza Drive—shown on these pages—is an imaginative fusion of space on a tight, precipitous plot on the hills above West Hollywood. Cascading down the hill, the house is dug into the site, and entered from the upper floor at street level. It

has been senstively restored in the spirit of the original architecture by Marmol and Radziner.

In the following passage, Lamprecht captures the house's unique style: "The facade is clearly assigned two roles, addressing private and public functions. The glass public entry, transparent to the view beyond, lies between the carport and the private wing. The carport's deep overhang is supported by stainless-steel-wrapped, chrome-plated tubular columns, while a white wall cuts off the view to the master bedroom stepping back; here the redwood sheathing now runs horizontally below clerestories. The carport, with a private door leading to the kitchen, doubles as an outdoor living space and enhances the sociability and cheerfulness of the house."

On the rear garden side, a long balcony and deck are accessible from both the living space and master bedroom. Sliding glass doors divide the deck from the interior spaces, so that the deck becomes an extension of the living area in warm weather. The overhanging roof offers additional shade and shelter. Ingenious and

ABOVE, ABOVE RIGHT, AND RIGHT The hilly topography of the site means that the house could be designed to be tucked into the slope, providing the occupants with both privacy and good views. It opens up at the rear, overlooking a garden and the wider city beyond. The architect's interiors reveal his skill in delicately layering spatial transitions. In this case, the entire city becomes a backdrop for the daily dramas of domestic life.

LEFT The carport on the street side of the house doubles as an outdoor living area. Fine Venetian blinds screen it from the rest of the living accommodation.

Interiors have a spare yet elegant quality. Natural materials and simple furnishings and textures have been carefully chosen to enhance Richard Neutra's wonderfully realized interaction of fluid space and reflected light.

elegant details include the use of taut piano wires to separate the living room from the stairwell, a detail taken up in the rear balcony balustrades. The strong verticality of this detail is emphasized in the rhythm of the redwood siding.

Neutra's views on nature had important consequences for his dwellings. As Lamprecht comments, "Frank Lloyd Wright's architecture emphasized the hearth as the nucleus of the home. If there is a comparable sacred spot in a Neutra house, it is the terrace, preferably a terrace with radiant heating, so that the relationship between indoors and out becomes charged with ambiguity. The conventional opaque boundary between indoors and out must be reduced to a thin plane of glass so nothing can interfere in that potent and primal relationship,

whether the benign landscaping of suburbia, or the terrifying grandeur of the Swiss Alps.

Many of Neutra's houses present a closed face to the street, apart from a high strip of windows, opening out to gardens to the rear. Often, the hilly topography of the site provides privacy, enabling houses to be tucked into slopes, which also serves to maximize views.

Lamprecht notes that Neutra's interiors reveal his skill in orchestrating activities within spaces. "Just as Neutra layered spatial transitions, he also layered functions. As he once said, more hopefully than realistically, 'In our house, rooms have no names such as living, room, dining room, bedroom ... Rooms are portions of a great organic living space and pragmatically elastic.' This 'great living space' sounds very much like the Japanese concept of the *zashiki* or principal flexible room used for living, sleeping, and entertaining. In Neutra's hands, such architectural traditions are lyrically reinterpreted for the hedonistic lifestyles of Southern California."

THIS PICTURE
Long bands of glazing illuminate the master bedroom on the lower floor. In a reversal of the conventional layout, Neutra placed the living space on the upper level, with the bedroom below. The result is a plan that is lucid and logical, with free-flowing spaces.

ABOVE RIGHT
The style of furniture enhances the sense of modern elegance.

RIGHT The staircase linking the two levels of the house was designed in response to the sloping site.

Berthold Lubetkin designed the penthouse at Highpoint II as a home for himself. Influenced by Le Corbusier's rooftop apartment in Paris, Lubetkin introduced curved shapes into the roof in contrast to the straight lines of the main Highpoint building. The windows command panoramas of London and give access to the roof terraces that run all around the apartment. A long travertine shelf runs beneath the windows.

SYMPHONY IN CONCRETE

When Le Corbusier visited London in 1935, he was impressed by the Highpoint flats, the work of the Russian architect Berthold Lubetkin. Highpoint's construction was entirely of concrete, finished in dazzling white paint with jaunty balconies and long windows, which could be folded away completely, to the living rooms. A handful of similar buildings were built in London in the 1930s, aiming to combine convenience of internal planning with the excitement of an architectural vision of the future.

To devotees of modern architecture in England, the penthouse at Highpoint II, the second of a pair of 1930s apartment buildings in north London, is a mythical, even a sacred, space. The architect of the buildings, the mysterious and charismatic Russian Berthold Lubetkin, lived in the penthouse from the time of their completion, shortly before World War II, until retiring to the country in the 1950s.

The penthouse tested the boundaries of modern architecture, introducing layers of additional and contradictory meanings into what many people still regard as an over-functional, unpoetic style. It has been lovingly restored by its present owners, who bought it in 1996 and have shown an inspired devotion to the space, rejoicing in their good fortune at being able to live there.

Highpoint penthouse feels like London's rooftop. Since it did not need to fit into a structural grid like the apartments on the floors below, Lubetkin gave the roof a curved profile,

RIGHT The Highpoint penthouse is entered through the door behind the pillar. The low ceiling provides an intimate sitting area around a fireplace covered with vertical pine boarding, one of many recreated features in this famous and unique space. Light comes mysteriously down onto the display shelf, where ceramics from the 1930s meet an African wood sculpture.

ABOVE Another African sculpture, standing on a bench next to the fireplace, is camouflaged by the pine boarding.

LEFT Contemporary furniture by one of the owners has the kind of solidity that makes it look entirely at home in the apartment. "If you can't lift it, it's designed by me," he says.

RIGHT Lubetkin chose to decorate the outside of the kitchen wall with Pollock toy theater prints, a form of Victorian folk art. The wall is now restored with authentic copies of the originals, full of soldiers, sailors, harlequins, and maids in distress. Since the prints fit the walls exactly, he must have conceived the idea at an early stage.

creating a high space in the center as well as a feeling of enclosure. When a strong wind is blowing, it can seem to people in the penthouse as if they are caught in a storm at sea.

In addition to smooth plaster on concrete, the architect introduced wall paneling of rough-riven pine, evoking the atmosphere of a log cabin in the wilderness. This shaggy quality was echoed in the suite of furniture he designed specially for the penthouse.

Much of the interior has had to be restored in recent years, drawing on the skill and knowledge of Lubetkin's biographer, the architect John Allan. The process began even before the present owners moved in; but thanks to their meticulous restoration, features of the interior—both originals and copies—are returning one by one.

Notable among the original features—and perhaps the most eccentric gesture in a supposedly modern interior—was the use of hand-colored cutout sheets for Pollock's toy theaters as wallpaper on the wall between the kitchen and the original dining area. These popular Victorian prints were still available in the 1930s from Benjamin Pollock's shop in Hoxton,

ABOVE RIGHT Emerging directly from the elevator, visitors remove their shoes by the bench—one of the few original features to have survived. Pine logs make a baffle, half concealing the view to the west. The tile pattern runs through the main rooms.

RIGHT A work space with an Eames chair has been installed in a corner of the main room. The recreated bookshelves are just behind.

BELOW Period lighting has been subtly used to add warmth and depth to the living space.

Lubetkin's individual combination of elements from 1938 has inspired a gradual reconstruction of his vision, but it is a flexible formula that allows other design influences to assert themselves.

London. Staff at Pollock's Toy Museum, its successor, found the same sheets that Lubetkin had originally used. Next to these, the original shelf units have been recreated, with their deep red background color, found after scraping the wall, which complements the restored original blue of the ceiling.

The penthouse is not simply a museum reconstruction, however, but reflects the taste of the owners, one of whom is a painter, the other a designer and maker of furniture. Fortunately, the diversity of style in the original design of the penthouse makes it receptive to objects of almost any character. For example, the chunky new furniture in the living area relates well to the tile grid while contrasting with the period furniture nearby. The owners say that their understanding of visual style has been utterly changed by the experience of living in a space that is continually revealing new subtleties of design.

ABOVE LEFT AND RIGHT The bathroom has been recreated in its original position with tiles the color of an old architectural blueprint.

LEFT AND RIGHT A discreet white door in one corner of the living space slides back to reveal the bedroom. Like the rest of the apartment, it is sparsely furnished. The dominant feature is an Eames chair, La Chaise of 1948, which was put into production by Vitra only in 1990.

RETRO REDEFINED

Every city embodies layers of civilization, not only in its design and architecture, but also in the arts and artifacts that its inhabitants embrace as their own. As the 20th century drew to a close, however, lifestyle trends seemed to fold back on themselves, reverting to nostalgia for the mid-century that persists to this day. In the early days of the Modern Retro boom, mid-century furnishings could be picked up for a song. Gradually, they have risen in value; at auction, classics of the 1940s and 1950s (and now even those of the 1960s and 1970s) fetch prices that compete with fine pieces from virtually every era. Furnishings by such luminaries as Charles and Ray Eames, Arne Jacobsen, George Nelson, and Florence Knoll have attained the status of icons. Such furnishings suit the slightly edgy urban settings at the forefront of contemporary design. Since collectors of mid-century furnishings frequently collect art, too, shape, texture, and color play off against each other in spirited dialogue. As in society, it's all about connections and who you know.

LEFT It would be hard to determine from its graffiti-smudged exterior that this former Brooklyn school contains the home and studio of gallery owner Evan Snyderman and his fiancée, Gabrielle Shelton.

OPPOSITE A long hall separates the living area from the studios and two bedrooms. Paintings by Snyderman's former tenant Jason Spivak line one wall; the window on the opposite wall looks into one of the studios. At the far end is a chair designed by Marc Held in 1970 for Knoll; the chair was in production for only a couple of months, making it very rare.

RECYCLED SCHOOLHOUSE

When Public School 52 was erected in 1890, it was one of the earliest public buildings to be built in the otherwise almost rural Bushwick section of Brooklyn. A century later, the building had been long abandoned. Windows were filled in with cement, utilities were nonexistent, and the place was filled with construction rubble, including old beams and bathtubs. Despite the ravages of the years, though, the building bore a certain dignity, and because it had been solidly built, it was structurally sound.

ABOVE The public space in the loft is furnished, sparingly, with mid-century pieces that have personal meaning for the owners. For example, the serpentine modular seating was designed by Donald Chadwick for Herman Miller in 1970, the year Evan was born. Hanging over it is a globe lamp by George Nelson, who also designed the clock. A low cabinet designed in the 1940s by Florence Knoll stands under the clock. The yellow plastic chair is by Wendell Castle; the painting is by Jason Spivak.

LEFT Evan's finest "trash pick" is a plywood chair by Charles Eames.

Seven years ago, when Evan Snyderman, a glassblower and sculptor, decided to relocate from Philadelphia to New York, he made forays to Williamsburg, Brooklyn, the new "SoHo" that was attracting artists unable to afford space in Manhattan's original SoHo. But even Williamsburg was expensive. Then he heard about the schoolhouse in Bushwick.

Snyderman knew he wanted plenty of space, and P.S. 52 certainly offered that: 5,000 square feet (465 square meters) on one full floor, with ceilings 14 feet (4.25 meters) high. Despite the loft's derelict condition, he decided to take a chance on it, trusting its landlord to upgrade the raw space and render it habitable within a reasonable amount of time.

He made a deal for a long-term lease, and, bundling his possessions under a tarp in the center of the space, moved in—even though

ABOVE The dining area in the main room is furnished with street finds, including an old American pine farm table and a pair of vintage Arne Jacobsen chairs. The triangular cabinet standing against the far wall came from Evan's parents' crafts gallery in Philadelphia; it originated in a hardware store and still bears the word CARBORUNDUM on one side. The monoprints are by Evan. The arc lamp is a reproduction.

LEFT One of the objects Jason Spivak left behind is a polka-dotted vase from the 1950s. The cigarette holder, which also dates from the 1950s, is Danish.

the windows remained blocked up. For six months, he camped out in this "black hole." Finally, the landlord traded cement for plywood at the windows, piercing each slab to bring in light; he also connected the necessary utilities.

While this was going on, Jason Spivak, a painter friend living in London, called Snyderman and asked if he could stay in the loft while he looked for a place to live. It turned out Spivak had worked as a contractor. He suggested that he and Snyderman undertake the remodeling themselves. Together, they erected sheetrock walls to define two bedrooms, two studios, and baths, all accessed by a long hall—leaving a third of the overall space for a spacious living and dining area. (A third studio lies outside the loft.) A kitchen steps up at one end of the living zone, in a space that may have been the principal's office. The men also revived brick walls, and they painted the scarred wood floors with multiple coats of high-gloss battleship-gray paint.

Once Spivak moved on, after a year of continuous work on the place, Snyderman secured a tenant for the outside studio. He also began to furnish the loft, mainly with pieces picked up in the street. An ardent "dumpster diver and trash picker," he regularly scavenged material to use in his sculptures. Sometimes,

RIGHT A pair of oak doors 10 feet (3 meters) high, which Snyderman found in Philadelphia, were installed in the entrance bay leading into his studio. One of his monoprints, *One Way*, hangs over a Marc Held chair and a diminutive Tulip occasional table by Eero Saarinen.

LEFT A rosewood chest from George Nelson's Thin Edge series for Herman Miller stands next to the bed. Drawer knobs are porcelain; legs are turned aluminum. The faded patina of brick blushes in the glow of a Laurel lamp.

BELOW A section of scaffolding stands in for a closet.

The loft was originally furnished with an array of items picked up in the street, including one outstanding treasure: a plywood chair by Charles Eames.

too, he came upon some real treasures, such as a plywood chair by Charles Eames, which dated to the mid-20th century. He began to concentrate exclusively on furniture from the era, becoming so infatuated with the style that he started up a business, the R 20th Century gallery, based in Manhattan's Tribeca.

Slowly, the loft became not only habitable, but homey. Snyderman's girlfriend, Gabrielle Shelton, a welder, moved in; now they are engaged. Together, the couple installed cabinets and counters in the kitchen (after the photos taken for these pages). And, as Evan unearths new and finer furnishings, the couple upgrades their collection, learning more and more as they do so. Which is, after all, the purpose of a school, too.

OPPOSITE The entrance hall is dominated by La Chaise, designed in 1948 by Charles and Ray Eames for an international competition of low-cost furniture. It lounges beneath a sculpture by Brad Dunning composed of three velvet cushions atop an aluminum box emblazoned with the nameplate from a 1950s Chrysler Imperial.

ABOVE AND RIGHT The television room has been left fundamentally as it was, except for the addition of new, red-leather seating and a 1950s accent table from France.

MODERN RETRO

In art, as in life, timing is everything—as demonstrated by the owner of this 6,000 square foot (560 square meter) apartment with wraparound terrace in one of Manhattan's prized addresses overlooking Central Park. Savvy financial investments over four decades allowed him to retire early, and acquire a vast collection of art. He also invested in mid-century modern furniture—before most dealers were even aware it might be the next best thing.

RIGHT The living room received the most thorough makeover. A large painting from 1974 by Robert Natkin stands out against plaster walls pigmented with burnt sienna, red, and yellow. Every piece is the room was brought in "new." Tufted reproduction Josef Hoffman couches sit on a rug specially colored by Michael d'Arcy to echo hues in the furnishings and art.

LEFT Pride of place belongs to the 6-foot (1.8-meter) long Mesa coffee table by T. H. Robsjohn-Gibbings. Behind it are two other rarities: a 1957 Arne Jacobsen Swan chair covered in period chartreuse boucle and a curvy sofa that was one of six prototypes designed by Isamu Noguchi and made by Herman Miller as Christmas presents for their senior executives. The red fabric is a Paul Klee pattern.

Faster than you can blink an eye, what is trendy becomes *passé*, then *outré*, then retro—and then, *voilà*, it's trendy once again. Such is the staying power of mid-century modern, though, that, once individual furnishings flitted onto the radar screen, the finest pieces remained there, sought out by collectors, who enjoy the freedom and playfulness they represent.

Apartments also succumb to vagaries of fashion. By the mid-1990s, this one had sunk into torpor. Its owner, a philanthropist involved with a number of institutions that support the arts, had settled into his apartment for the long haul and hadn't particularly noticed that the place was showing its age. Over the years, John Stewart, a painter and art consultant who had curated all of the artworks in the apartment, had encouraged his friend to refresh the space. What finally persuaded the art collector to do so was a two-pronged plan: together with a designer and friend, the late Michael d'Arcy, Stewart would

FAR LEFT TOP A vivid yellow Coconut chair by George Nelson, dated 1955, stands between a case with drawers from the 200 series of storage units by Charles Eames and Arne Jacobsen's Swan loveseat. The cork-top coffee table with splayed mahogany legs is by Paul Frankel.

FAR LEFT BOTTOM The pinched bottle with stopper is by Avem.

LEFT Michael d'Arcy crafted this lamp's tiered silk lampshade.

not only make the place more comfortable and, he says, "visually exciting," he would also create an environment that would remind the owner "of when he came of age, both personally and financially—the 1950s."

Intrigued with Stewart's proposal, the collector gave his go-ahead—to redo the living room only, on a tight budget. For two months, Stewart and d'Arcy combed New York antique stores, buying individual mid-century pieces for modest prices. Partway through the process, they discovered a coffee table by T. H. Robsjohn-Gibbings that so bowled them over that they confronted the collector in what Stewart terms a "budget-

ABOVE LEFT Like the TV room, the dining room was left virtually untouched, except for new upholstery on the Lucite chairs; even the Venetian chandelier stayed put. Ed Paschke's Mona Lisa series gazes upon the dining table and chairs designed by Vladimir Kagan, which have occupied this room since they were new, in the 1970s. The rug is by Andrée Putman, with color arrangements by Michael d'Arcy.

ABOVE John Stewart hung one of his own paintings above a rare steel-framed storage piece by George Nelson for Herman Miller.

LEFT The striated hanging lamps are by Massimo Vignelli for Venini.

Today, the apartment feels so comfortable that the owner is almost unaware that any changes have been made. To achieve that effect is an art in itself.

busting" discussion. Persuaded of its importance, the owner cried "damn the budget!" and gave Stewart and d'Arcy carte blanche to negotiate for top-quality pieces, not only for the living room, but for the rest of the apartment as well.

Once they had assembled the furnishings, the pair presented their next "tough sell": to perfect the backdrops for the art. Again, the collector had to be persuaded; again he deferred to their judgment. Stewart and d'Arcy removed wall moldings where necessary, then worked with pigments and Venetian plaster, which contains crushed marble and other minerals, to achieve a pearlescent finish. Finally, they moved the paintings around to show them off to their best advantage.

FAR LEFT Walls between the windows in the main living area, which bear remnants of old coats of paint, have been scrubbed down and polished to bring out their varying tonalities. A refurbished structural column anchors the space; "everything spins out from there," says owner John Cheim. The maple, scroll-arm bench is 7 feet (2.1 meters) long; it is French, as are the 1930s rope-and-wood chairs. The nesting tables are nickel.

INSET CENTER Wake, the golden labrador, snoozes on an Edward Wormley bench.

LEFT The circular tripod table is by T. H. Robsjohn-Gibbings.

AN ARTISTIC ATTITUDE

New York City has often been described as a collection of villages. Some of these are residential districts, while others are dedicated to light manufacturing. Each embodies a character and aura all its own. The area that adjoins the Flatiron Building—immortalized in a famous snowy photograph of 1905 by Edward Steichen—is a neighborhood that has long produced inexpensive versions of upscale accessory items such as gloves, belts, and handbags. Just to the west lies the so-called Flower District, where wholesale blooms and plants are sold, while to the north and east of the building and of Madison Square Park the silver, china, and glass industries and the children's toy market maintain showrooms.

OPPOSITE A diptych by Joan Mitchell hangs behind a burl-top table by Robsjohn-Gibbings, who also designed the table in the foreground. Mitchell was inspired by sunflowers, which she watched "as if they were human," Cheim says.

ABOVE One of John Cheim's design ploys was to break up the loft's rectangular spaces with circular tables; the largest is a boardroom table by Florence Knoll. On it stands a Bauer vase; beyond is an abstract painting from the mid-1980s by Richmond Burton.

ABOVE, INSET Chairs surrounding the table are from Steelcase. The print is by Jean-Michel Basquiat.

LEFT An Louise Fischman abstract hangs over a daybed by Alvar Aalto.

This loft in the Flatiron district, which belongs to art-gallery owner John Cheim, once functioned as a sweatshop for the assembly of handbags. When Cheim looked out his windows, he could see workers hunched over sewing machines in buildings across the way. During the past two decades, the Flatiron area has opened up to other industries, notably publishing, advertising, and public relations, plus the professions that support them, such as graphics and photography.

Despite the influx of white-collar business, it was some time before many people sought out the area as a place to live. When John arrived in 1982, the neighborhood was still considered "a nowhere spot," he says. The biggest excitement from those early years was the opening of a delicatessen at the corner of his block. Today, the neighborhood is hip and fashionable, amply sprinkled with boutiques and restaurants.

LEFT Cheim designed the platform bed that stands in front of a 1960 painting by Joan Mitchell. Picture shelves showcase smaller prints and drawings. Beneath them is an African chair. The bronze head on the glass-topped table is by Alice Neel.

THIS PICTURE Located in the center of the loft is a galley-style kitchen, where the focus is on a collection of art pottery, much of which came from the late-lamented 26th Street Flea Market, a must-visit site for many collectors. The red jar on the counter is a Catalina.

FAR RIGHT TOP The stools came from the 26th Street market.

FAR RIGHT BOTTOM Cheim likes the lamp on the Art Deco marble table because its base suggests a torso. Next to it is an African mask.

In redesigning the apartment, one aim was to recapture the wide open landscapes of the owner's youth.

Cheim, who grew up in California and Colorado, initially came to New York from the Rhode Island School of Design (RISD) with the intention of being a painter. To earn his keep, he took a job at the Drawing Center in SoHo, and, from there, moved over to the Robert Miller gallery, where he remained for 20 years, in time becoming its director.

While Cheim was at Robert Miller, his best friend from RISD, Howard Read, joined the gallery as a specialist in photography. In 1996, the two men got together and opened their own space, Cheim & Read, in the heart of the up-and-coming Chelsea art district. In October 2001, they moved into a dramatic new space on West 25th Street, just steps from the Hudson River.

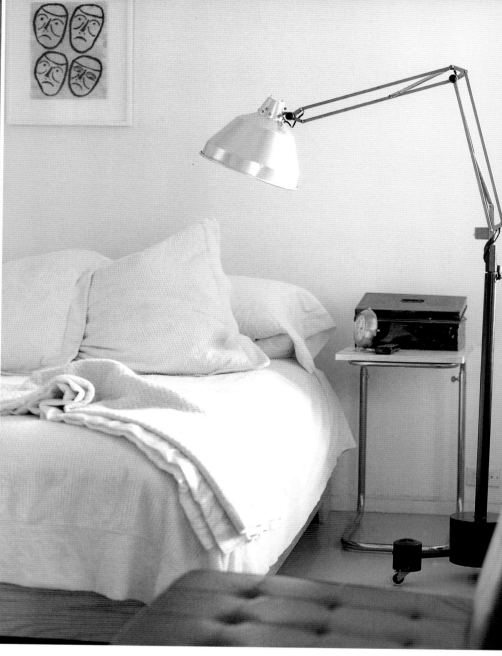

John Cheim always conceived of his loft as an ancillary gallery space. Working with architect John Williams, he gutted it, then smoothed the surfaces. With 12-foot (3.7-meter) high ceilings and an abundance of light, the 4,500-square-foot (420-square-meter) space allows him both to showcase large-scale paintings, as well as to accommodate his collection of American art pottery, plus small works of sculpture, drawings, and prints. Walls are configured to create broad vistas, so works of art can be appreciated from the long view as well as up close. The old wooden floors are sheathed with plywood, which Williams slicked with layers of durable liquid epoxy for a seamless look. The glowing epoxy "throws up light so everything seems to float in the space," Cheim says.

The art he collects—much of it in an abstract expressionistic vein—emanates from his interest in nature, too. "These are paintings that cannot be contained in one 'shot' so you can always see something new in them."

The space is configured so that works of art can be appreciated from the long view.

OPPOSITE A desk and chairs from the 1940s by Alvar Aalto adorn the office, in front of a wall of storage. Works by Louise Bourgeois, Andy Warhol, and Diane Arbus are shown on the shelf. The box is by Jean-Michel Basquiat.

ABOVE LEFT In the bathroom, the illustration of sea sponges comes from Paris. The 1930s sink is from Urban Archaeology, a prime architectural salvage source.

ABOVE A Ronald Baecheler hangs in the second bedroom.

RIGHT This metal and plastic webbed chair was designed in the 1950s to be used poolside at the Howard Johnson's chain of motels and eateries.

SPIRIT OF THE SIXTIES

This elegant penthouse in one of the lower-rise buildings of London's Barbican complex—built in the 1960s by the architects Chamberlin, Powell & Bon—features a barrel-vaulted concrete roof that vastly increases the sense of interior space.

OPPOSITE The Barbican apartment is simply and appropriately furnished, recreating the mood of the original late 1960s period. The projecting strip of wood at the junction of the wall and vault conceals miniature strip lighting that throws light up onto the curve of the roof.

THIS PAGE: MAIN PICTURE Lightweight and comfortable Eames chairs are a prominent feature of this apartment, which is devoid of clutter.

THIS PAGE: INSET The view east gives glimpses of the ever-changing skyline of the City of London.

A strong architectural statement, inextricably linked with the 1960s, has been harmoniously amplified, and extra elements added in the spirit of the original.

The Barbican complex in the City of London is a place that tends to divide opinion sharply (see also pages 156–61). Outsiders often find it hard to navigate through and around the tall residential towers and apartment buildings, which are linked by a series of terraces and walkways overlooking areas of garden and lake. For residents, however, the Barbican offers the convenience of living right in the middle of London with many local facilities, including a theater, cinema, concert hall, and exhibition gallery. These aspects particularly appealed to a Belgian couple seeking a London base. They were lucky enough to find a penthouse apartment in one of lower buildings. It had been rented for many years, and although some of the original features remained, it needed careful updating to meet the needs of the new owners. They entrusted the job to Jo Hagan of USE Architects, whose refit combines elegance and practicality.

ABOVE Kitchen fixtures have been lovingly preserved, including the stainless-steel sink and the recessed burners on the rear wall with its high-level knobs. Elegant glass-fronted storage cupboards have been added in a style that complements the original fixtures.

LEFT Double doors allow the kitchen to be incorporated into the living room or shut away completely as required. The dining table is a version of Eero Saarinen's classic design with a teak top.

RIGHT Huge windows slide open to give access to a small balcony area.

RIGHT AND FAR RIGHT Several years ago, the apartment's new owners inserted a mezzanine level in the apartment to create a bed platform, which is accessed by steep cantilevered steps. Slits in the underside of the platform provide ventilation for the bed base overhead. A useful workspace has been created underneath the bed platform, on the level of the former bedroom, which has been elegantly equipped with roomy shelves and storage drawers, as well as a small desk.

The apartment is a long rectangle in plan with windows at each end. An outside stairway arrives at the midpoint of one side, giving access to a narrow passage leading into the main room with its a spectacular barrel-vaulted concrete roof. Wood-framed windows open onto a wide, south-facing balcony. One wall is papered in Japanese grass-cloth, giving a warmth of texture and tone that is authentic to the period of the building. A small work desk is built into a wall recess.

The kitchen lies behind the back wall and is accessed by flush-fitting double doors. The owners wanted to keep the original steel sink, but they have added a new counter on the opposite wall. The kitchen has skylight windows only, but they offer a glimpse of sky through an arched opening in the concrete wall outside. Backing onto the kitchen is the bathroom, which also retains most of its original features.

At the rear of the apartment, a mezzanine platform has been inserted, reached by a steep flight of wooden steps that are a sculptural feature in their own right. The bed is a simple mattress on the floor, with concealed lighting panels at the head and foot, and a low guard rail where the platform meets the ladder stair.

Sheltered underneath the mezzanine is a practical storage unit, neatly detailed in a style. The simple device of moving the original glazed panel beside the door a couple of feet into the hallway has made the new space both larger and more interesting. In the hall, two windows open onto the brightly lit top of the stairwell, giving borrowed light to what would otherwise be the dark central zone of the apartment.

The Eames Aluminum chairs and Saarinen Tulip dining suite were already in the possession of the present owners, whose home town is the European manufacturing center for Knoll International, original makers of these pieces.

LEFT The bathroom is a miniature version of the monumentality of the Barbican, with a sink solidly built into a concrete tiled top. The mirrors and towel rods are all original fixtures, including a medicine cabinet and a small mirror panel on the side wall, which creates an all-round view and increases the sense of light and space.

OPPOSITE The bed platform is reached by a wooden ladder stair, slotted in beside a new closet space. Above is a delightful sleeping area, light and airy, with a feeling of being close to the sky. Underneath, a sleek and understated desk teamed with an Eames Aluminum Group chair leaves plenty of floor space.

The kitchen and bathroom, both lit by high windows, are "secret" spaces in which many original features have been preserved.

HEIGHT OF LUXURY

The striking concrete blocks of the Barbican, within a stone's throw of St. Paul's Cathedral in the City of London, were officially opened in 1969. The complex was designed to cater specifically for City professionals, and its compact apartments featured all mod cons. From the outside, the monolithic structures can seem bleak and unwelcoming, but the apartment interiors reveal a dramatic contrast, where effortless function and elegant luxury come together to create chic and comfortable homes.

LEFT The towers of the Barbican estate are an imposing presence on the city's skyline.

RIGHT Bredenbeck made a library and office from what had been two small bedrooms; his own bedroom is at the end of the hall. The brown walls of the office bring out the rich color and grain of his rosewood furniture, which includes a chair, a table, and an elegant cabinet.

OPPOSITE, INSET The tea set on the table is by Branksome China and is very rare.

High-rise living does not appeal to everybody—but it is an odd fact that the phrase "tower block" conjures up one mental image, while "penthouse suite" has an entirely different effect. Kurt Bredenbeck's 38th-floor Barbican apartment isn't quite a penthouse, but with its lovely views, incomparable amenities, and slick decoration, it might as well be.

"It's my ideal hotel suite," says Bredenbeck, who, as a hotel entrepreneur, ought to know what he's talking about. "I've got a 24-hour doorman, underground parking, cable TV and ISDN, and people deliver. And the building is very solid, so you can't hear anybody around you."

Distinctive design elements include beautiful hardwood door and window frames, neatly aligned light switches, placed at just the right height, and a combined footbath–shower–bidet that fits neatly into the small bathroom. The place has been maintained immaculately over the years, so that all the original fixtures are as good as new.

It was this strongly period atmosphere that gave Bredenbeck his decorative theme: "IBM executive, circa 1970." He had planned to rip everything out and install sliding doors and a new

OPPOSITE, ABOVE LEFT Bredenbeck bought the rosewood cabinet in Brick Lane market—it was designed in the 1970s by a British firm, Merrow Associates. The side chair is by Charles and Ray Eames, but the armchairs are modern, made to Bredenbeck's specifications (he wanted leather in just the color of Knoll's famous tan).

OPPOSITE, ABOVE RIGHT Another striking rosewood cabinet, also by Merrow Associates, is flanked by a Le Corbusier hide-covered chair. The lamp on the sideboard is by Verner Panton.

OPPOSITE, BELOW LEFT The side table in the living room is by Arkana of Bath, inspired by Eero Saarinen.

OPPOSITE, BELOW RIGHT This George Nelson shelving system is rarely found in rosewood. Bredenbeck bought it at auction and it fits perfectly into his office. The Corbusier armchairs are unusually heavy—they came from the *QE2* liner.

RIGHT The kitchen units remain exactly as they were in 1969. In a tiny dining area at the far end, an Eames table is matched with a 1940s sofa and Marcel Breuer dining chairs.

The background decor is quietly complementary to the designer pieces, with the rich grain and color of antique wood offset by soft tan leather, cream wool curtains, and warm brown walls.

LEFT An efficient corner storage cupboard, the sculptural Tizio reading lights, and the coolly enveloping midnight-blue walls emphasize the bedroom's masculine character. The bed was made in Italy and covered with a Knoll fabric, as was the wire Diamond chair by Harry Bertoia, a design produced by Knoll from the early 1950s.

ABOVE The rosewood side table is an Eames. The lovely pot that has been placed on it is, perhaps surprisingly, from Denby. The reading light, designed in 1972 by Richard Sapper, is a modern classic.

kitchen, but settled on a solution that was both more economical and more in keeping with the building's architecture. He converted two small bedrooms into one large office, then set about collecting mid-century designer furniture.

Bredenbeck particularly loves rosewood, which he began buying years before it became fashionable. He started with the 1970s sideboard that dominates the living room, adding further pieces as he came across them, including a dining table used as a desk and a rare shelving system by George Nelson. Designer names are all around, from the Bertoia chair in the bedroom to the Corbusier armchairs in the library, mingled with elegant Chinese ceramics and the occasional retro accessory. It's all seriously high quality, and about as far from the typical notion of tower-block living as it is possible to get.

RELAXED ECLECTIC

For some city-lovers, the allure of the urban environment is closely allied with the exciting cornucopia of thrift-store and flea-market finds that have taken up residence in their homes. Indeed, those people who feel most comfortable with a relaxed eclectic lifestyle tend to follow the muse of serendipity—mixing old and new, plain and arcane, with whimsy and flair. The dedicated urbanites whose homes are featured in this chapter are united by conspicuous independence of spirit. Their flights of fancy are exemplified by a child's swing in a penthouse kitchen —which allows its owner to enjoy some gentle therapy while the coffee brews. More startling are the aluminum nuts-and-bolts-studded sides of a panelized container truck—used to make partitions between the private and public spaces of a loft. One panel conceals a television, which can be gracefully pivoted into position when its owners want to catch a flick in bed. Another apartment, in Paris, has an outdoor shower on the roof – with a view like that, who care if it rains?

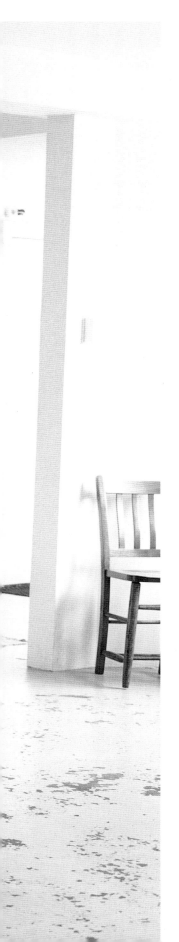

WATERSIDE WAREHOUSE

Along the picturesque canals of old Amsterdam, you can escape the feel of city life altogether and imagine yourself in a timeless place of calm and quiet. The same atmosphere imbues the homes of two artistic sisters, who live on separate floors of the same building overlooking the Lijnbaans Canal. Furnished with simple, pretty, country antiques and painted in cool, pale colors, these light and airy homes have no set "style," just effortless ease and unassuming tranquility.

OPPOSITE There are few walls in the sisters' apartments, creating a spacious and airy feel. Here, in typically relaxed style, Aleid Röntgen uses garden chairs around a circular dining table. The patinated floor was a happy accident: layers of paint peeled away gradually, resulting in a variegated effect that she and her husband love.

BELOW The former clock factory is occupied by around 40 artists, architects, sculptors, and musicians. It overlooks the Lijnbaans Canal.

E very city has areas where artists gather—often where rents are low and properties spacious and light enough to make practical studios. And, slowly, a forgotten backwater becomes a desirable enclave buzzing with creative endeavor. One such area is Jordaan in Amsterdam, also famous for its flea market and farmers' market; at its heart is a former clock factory housing forty or so apartments lived in by artists, architects, sculptors, and musicians. Mainly graduates from Amsterdam's Royal School of Art, they pooled resources in 1982 to buy the whole building, and converted it into individual homes, each designed around their personal needs, but all with a loft-style feel.

Sisters Annette Brederode and Aleid Röntgen own a unit each on the second and third floors; although they have separate entrances, they love living so close to each other. Until recently, the sisters worked together, too, holding twice-yearly sales of art and antiques in Annette Brederode's apartment. Brederode, a former art therapist, now concentrates on her own paintings and on running the sales, while Röntgen is a landscape

THIS PICTURE Both Aleid Röntgen and her husband love to entertain; he is a violinist and they sometimes hold concerts in the apartment. The dining table, flanked by a bench and mismatched chairs collected over the years, is slim but seats plenty of guests. Röntgen herself made the cotton curtains

RIGHT Annette Brederode's dining table is around 150 years old. She has arranged comfortable cotton rugs over the old wooden floors, providing warmth and soundproofing.

BELOW RIGHT The folding garden chair is typical of the pretty, informal furniture that Annette Brederode picks up on her regular buying trips to France. Antique bird cages such as these are becoming hard to find, but Brederode still has around 80 in her apartment. She has been collecting them since she was 15 and believes she has sold between 400 and 500 over the years.

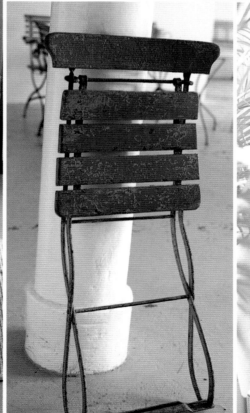

OPPOSITE Annette Brederode's kitchen consists of nothing more complicated than a row of painted-wood cupboards combined with open shelving. She stores her attractive kitchenware on top of the cupboards, creating an informal display.

LEFT The walls around Brederode's dining table are covered in tongue-and-groove boarding, contributing to the farmhouse effect. The mirror is a French antique, and the hanging lampshade is in a country style typical of both French and Dutch period lighting.

BELOW LEFT In a corner of Aleid Röntgen's living area is a simple basin low enough for her children to wash their hands and paintbrushes.

BELOW RIGHT Brederode collects enamelware, which she displays around the apartment on old-fashioned open shelves.

Against a backdrop of pale, painted walls and unfussy window treatments, the country-style pieces of furniture look all the prettier for their patina of age.

architect. Their professional lives complemented their living arrangements, as Brederode explains: "I started collecting antiques many years ago, and when my sister designs gardens, her clients often ask for nice furniture to put in them, so it was very natural to start working together."

Both apartments are open and spacious, with pale walls and unfussy window treatments, and the furniture is similarly unpretentious. For both sisters the overall look has hardly changed in 20 years. "We just did what we liked, without thinking about whether it was a trend or a style," says Röntgen. "We didn't have very much money, so we just tried to put nice things together in a very simple way." Simplicity is the secret to their success: without the straightjacket of style, these homes are highly personal, full of character and sublimely appealing.

PARIS EYRIE

The Eiffel Tower and the Panthéon—last resting place of many great Frenchmen—are among the landmarks that can be enjoyed from this rustic-style apartment that soars above the rooftops of Paris. The loftlike space is full of light and air, while the bustle below dissolves into a distant murmur.

The old wooden swing that hangs from the kitchen ceiling in this rooftop Paris apartment says it all. We are clearly in the company of people who dream of freedom— freedom from the restrictions of the city, freedom to be themselves, freedom to be children again.

The owner of the flat, with its breathtaking views over Paris, had always wanted a swing exactly the same as the one at her childhood home in County Cork, in the Republic of Ireland. But, provocatively, she wanted one inside her house. And she got it, here in the kitchen of this eyrie right in the heart of Paris. Surprisingly, the apartment is near the Gare du Nord—one

ABOVE Protected from the elements by a glass conservatory, the owners and their visitors can enjoy panoramas of Paris from the comfort of this colorful seating.

LEFT The living area at one end of the open-plan salon is occupied by a sofa and armchairs. The wooden floor is made of planks bought in London and salvaged from railroad carriages. The painted chest of drawers was rescued from a construction site in Ireland; above it hangs a collection of fishing rods.

FAR LEFT The inspired decision to install a rooftop shower makes bathing an invigorating experience. The parapet wall is enclosed in zinc, and the floor of the shower is the glass-block ceiling of the kitchen.

terminus of the Eurostar train—and only five minutes' walk from the Paris Opéra.

It was pure chance that persuaded the owner to live in Paris. A few years before moving to the city, one May, the Irish expatriate had come back to her London home from traveling in China and had found snow. Shortly afterward, she went to Paris for a weekend and saw that the sun was shining. She never returned.

The apartment now has four bedrooms, a kitchen-salon, and a rooftop terrace featuring an open-air shower. When she first discovered it, in the mid-1990s, it was divided into 13 small rooms. Pigeons were nesting in the airy space. The wind whistled through broken tiles in the roof. Now it is a comfortable home—a tribute to the power of the imagination, to ingenuity, and to sound common sense.

LEFT A massive antique French table and junk-shop chairs make an unusual combination.

FAR LEFT The views from the apartment include many of Paris's great landmarks, such as the Panthéon and the Eiffel Tower.

RIGHT The comfortable velvet-covered armchairs look warmly inviting.

BELOW In a corner of the apartment a spidery utilitarian metal floor lamp meets its match in an old, spartan, rust-spotted meal chair.

LEFT The kitchen, with its glass-block ceiling, is regularly flooded with light, while the swing, like so much else in the apartment, is recycled—consisting of bits of parquet left over from the floor. The mellow wood of the kitchen units comes from a church in Ireland. The backsplash is made of Belgian tiles, while the wall is decorated with German caricatures dating from World War I.

RIGHT Despite its size and sturdiness, the dining table has plenty of space around it in this airy apartment. Apart from a few striking ornaments, decoration is kept to a minimum and, as in other parts of the apartment, light floods in from all sides.

BELOW A sturdy wooden ladder increases the sense of light and space in the living room as well as making an unexpected and intriguing focal point.

The owner is a painter, photographer, and interior decorator, and her husband is an architect and photographer—for both of them, light was one of the most important factors in any living space. So, in no time at all after they moved in, three extra windows had been introduced into what was the servants' quarters of a 1930s building, and a glass-block ceiling had been installed above the kitchen. Ingeniously, the ceiling doubles as the floor of the rooftop shower. Not a single drop of water has ever seeped through to the kitchen.

The roof provides the owners of this apartment with ultimate escape—from the concrete jungle and from the busy-ness of life on the streets of Paris. From here they have a picture-postcard view of the capital city, and the Eiffel Tower is reflected in mirrors. With every shower of rain, the colors change. With every shift of light, Paris itself appears to change.

FAR LEFT An antique bed with wickerwork panels takes pride of place in the principal bedroom. The carving on the bed panels is the only concession to ornament, and the plainness of the surroundings emphasizes its intricacy.

LEFT AND BELOW On a cold day, taking a shower is a more modest affair than braving the rooftop alternative. The shower and basin occupy one corner of the bedroom. The tiles used on the floor are the same as those in the kitchen frieze, teamed with midnight-blue curtains.

If you are lucky enough to have lived in Paris in childhood or early adulthood, then wherever you go for the rest of your life, it stays with you—for Paris is a movable feast.

INDUSTRIAL CHIC

Schools, warehouses, churches, hospitals—in the eternal search for space in the city, it seems that any unused building is snapped up for conversion into a designer pad. What's unusual is for someone to take on a former factory and turn it into a home that is both fun and functional—which is just what a French photographer, with the help of an architect friend, has done here, creating an atmospheric space that is as comfortable as it is inspiring.

No one would rush to describe the apartment pictured here as a typical family home—but for the Morels that's exactly what it is. True, there is no fluffy carpet, matching sofa and chairs, or manicured lawn, but what they have instead is plenty of practical floor space that wears well and doesn't show the dirt, a range of furniture that is both interesting and comfortable, and a courtyard that brings the outdoors right into their living room.

The way the apartment looks and functions today is the result of a happy collaboration between the Morels and the architect François Muracciole. The Morels had bought a former factory in the lively Belleville and Republic area of Paris, once a small *atelier* that produced high-quality springs. It wasn't promising. There were only two windows in the entire building, and in some places there was dirt instead of floors.

LEFT Marie-Pierre Morel has added a lively note to the sitting area with a zebra-skin rug. The terracotta head is from Africa.

BELOW The wooden floors in the ground-floor living space are made from cheap pine, stained dark brown—they look as if they have been there for years. Two African ladders have been placed against the far wall; their carved wood contrasts beautifully with the hard metal found elsewhere in the apartment.

RIGHT The distressed shelving was found in a flea market. A collection of interesting objects sits on top, including a small spotlight from a cinema, a snow globe, and a fish vertebra. The black and white triptych on the wall behind is by Morel; it was taken with a pinhole camera and depicts a seashore and a road.

ABOVE The metal-framed windows that surround the courtyard were specially made.

LEFT The massive bookshelves were inspired by a small set of shelves discovered at a flea market.

FAR LEFT, ABOVE The old filing cabinet was found in the factory; the African wooden spoon has been mounted as if it were a precious object.

FAR LEFT, BELOW The photograph of a head is by Marie-Pierre Morel; an African wooden bowl sits on a stool that was also left in the factory.

RIGHT One of Morel's photographs provides the backdrop to the living space. Pieces of furniture include an old cabinet, two flea-market chairs, and a paper lamp by the designer Isamu Noguchi. The doorway to the left leads to the kitchen.

The big advantage, however, was the internal courtyard—roofed during the life of the factory—which had given the Morels the idea of creating an outside area in the middle of their apartment. Taking off the roof would give them much-needed light and an intriguing view. "They were worried about losing space, though," says Muracciole, "and they needed to be able to live there without it feeling like a warehouse. So we worked out a way of dividing it up using a mezzanine level and sliding metal-and-glass doors."

It became a flexible living space, with areas for work and play, reading and relaxation, plus two bedrooms and a kitchen, arranged around the bamboo-planted courtyard. Some parts are double-height, bright and spacious; others are tucked under the mezzanine, with a cozy feel. In the basement (once a coal cellar) is a spacious bathroom, while in the upper apartment is another bedroom and a shower room. "I wanted to keep the spirit of the place so it would still be the factory at heart," says Marie-Pierre Morel.

The most striking element of this home is its industrial spirit, from the stained-pine floorboards to the metal mezzanine, bookshelves, radiators, and lights. Muracciole used old metal beams left

MAIN PICTURE The building's industrial ethos is particularly apparent in the kitchen, which has a cast-concrete sink and work surface and unpainted, exposed pipework. The "artworks" in the background are actually X-rays of Marie-Pierre Morel's daughter's foot and chest.

LEFT Pipework and faucets are utterly basic yet highly appealing; a decorator friend of Morel's suggested the design.

OPPOSITE, LEFT The dining table was bought at a flea market in Provence. Morel believes that, since it is so ink-stained, it must have come from a school. The dining table has been teamed with a group of classic French metal café chairs.

ABOVE François Muracciole designed a zinc backsplash to complement the concrete work surfaces, re-using zinc from the building's original roof.

Flea-market pieces made from tough, robust materials have a no-frills feel that perfectly encapsulates the industrial ethos.

OPPOSITE **In the days when the building was a factory, what is now an upper-floor bedroom was a changing room for staff; the battered old door is a factory relic. The bed is a simple futon with a sky blue cover, and the floor—continuing the raw, tough, industrial theme—is bare concrete.**

ABOVE AND RIGHT The coal cellar was turned into a bathroom, where the only natural light comes from a glass block in the floor of the kitchen above. The walls have been left rough and bare, giving the feel of being carved out of the ground: Morel wanted it to resemble a Turkish hammam. The large stone sink—found in a flea market—was once used for making chocolate.

at the *atelier* to make the mezzanine, and was inspired in his design of the huge bookshelves by a flea-market find. As for the furniture, some was found abandoned in the old factory, and much of the rest came from flea markets, where Morel is a regular. Unsurprisingly, she is no fan of the over-decorated look, but she has included some attractive and highly individual displays of her own blown-up black-and-white photographs, various African artefacts, and quirky flea-market finds, which blend perfectly into her unusual home. Unpolished and unpretentious, the factory has been domesticated—but not diminished.

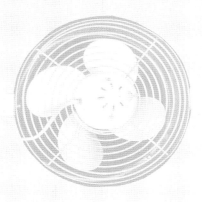

RIGHT The main loft space consists of an irregular rectangle with windows along one side, next to the relaxing and working area. Two adjacent square spaces provide a sleeping area at the back of the loft and a bathing area off to one side. Installing part of a container truck in this former commercial unit introduces a powerful industrial aesthetic and effectively divides the space into public and private areas.

FLEXIBLE LOFT

Recycling a container truck as a device to divide a single space may seem an extraordinary concept, but it provides an efficient, practical, and flexible architectural solution. Installing parts of the truck in a former commercial unit in midtown Manhattan imposes a powerful industrial aesthetic on a basic structural shell, unifies an irregular space, and subdivides a multifunctional living environment.

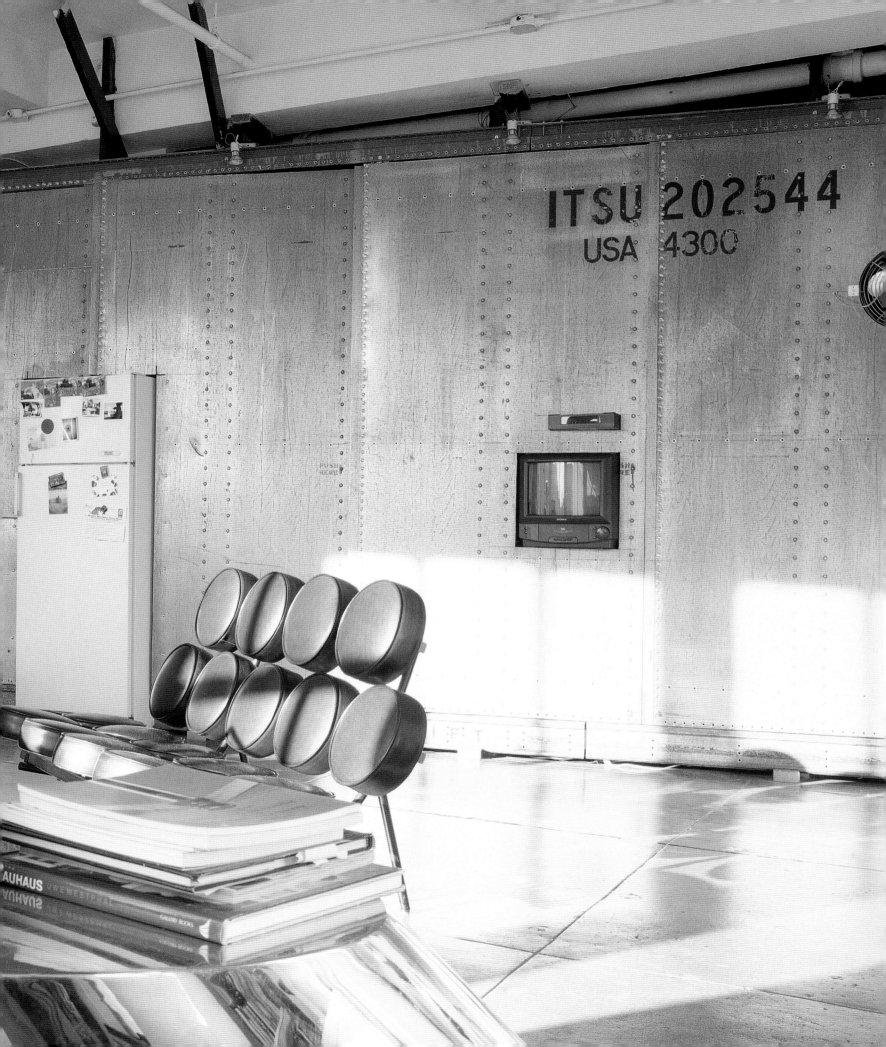

ABOVE, RIGHT, AND FAR RIGHT The side of the truck divides the space on a diagonal axis extending from beside the entrance straight through to the bathing zone. In the kitchen area, different sections of the truck siding flip up to reveal appliances and zones for cooking and food preparation.

LEFT Incorporating a television and video recorder into the aluminum truck divider serves to underline its involvement in the day-to-day activities of the loft.

A photographer and a designer of theatrical sets together took on this former commercial unit in Manhattan with the intention of developing a versatile open-plan living and working environment. In common with many open-plan, multifunctional environments, the challenge was how to organize the space, prioritize and integrate activities, and incorporate adequate provisions for screening off different areas. In this case—involving a New York couple with a keen visual and design sense—a private sleeping area on view to visiting clients would have been inappropriate, whereas a large work table that hijacks much of the main living area is considered entirely acceptable.

The space itself—a rectangle with a large square added on at the back and a smaller one at the side—suggests a convenient and logical division into front-of-house and back-of-house activities. Also, positioning everyday appliances, such as the shower, kitchen sink, and stove, along a single axis, simplifies division and separation. For the architects, establishing this single axis became the starting point for an inventive installation in keeping with their

commitment to recycling industrial cast-offs. The aluminum siding from what was once a container truck has been incorporated into the loft. It effectively intersects the space at a diagonal, drawing a highly visible and assertive line between public and private areas.

The aluminum truck siding is cut into a number of different moving sections—all of which flip up, pivot, or rotate to reveal different functions or areas within the space. The sections give the impression of being rough and heavy, yet the mechanisms that control them are precise and efficient, meaning that no exertion is required to lift and open individual sections. The ease of operation promotes flexibility and manipulation of space.

A wooden frame props up the aluminum siding like a billboard and supports horizontal aluminum beams or rails running along the top and bottom of the siding. In the kitchen, two flip-up sections conceal the cooking and food preparation areas, with a cupboard door over the sink. Operating independently or together, the sections provide

RIGHT The side of the container truck divides the loft diagonally into front-of-house working and relaxing areas and back-of-house sleeping and bathing zones. The kitchen area and appliances are part and parcel of the diagonal axis itself.

ABOVE The panel containing the television screen swings open to reveal a bedroom. Conveniently, the screen is visible from the bed.

LEFT Separating the living and sleeping areas, three independent sections of the truck siding spin in the manner of swing doors, offering easy access and multiple variations of openness. The truck sections look rough and heavy, but the mechanisms that control them are precise and efficient.

RIGHT Recycling old commercial filing cabinets and lockers provides a wall of comprehensive storage.

various combinations or degrees of openness. When all the sections are shut, an abstract line-up of appliances protrudes from the aluminum. However, frequency of use means that all or part of the kitchen usually remains open, providing vibrant background color.

The truck sections that separate the bedroom from the living space operate like swing doors, and can easily be opened and closed. Changing the position of the middle section controls the angle of the built-in video and television.

The front-of-house area is a flexible living and working area, with the emphasis firmly on working. The central focus is one large workstation on wheels that contains everything relating to work. In theory the table can be moved, but in practice it is the center of activity.

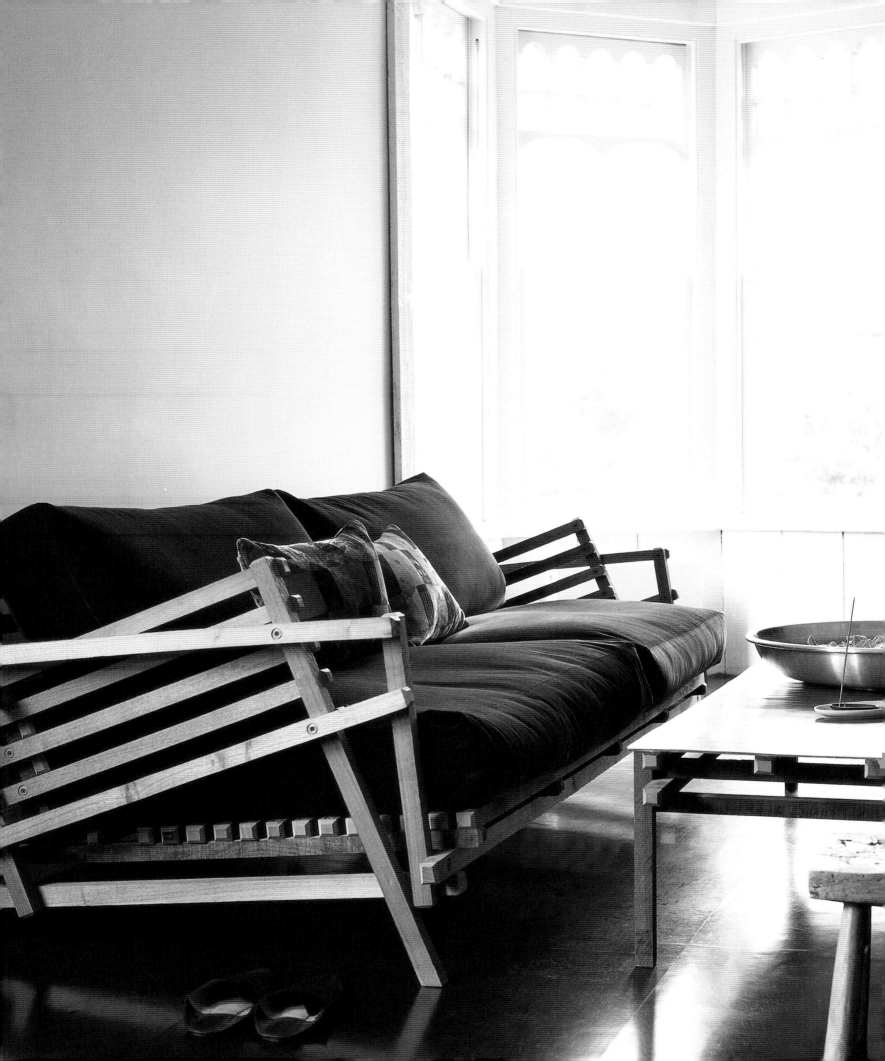

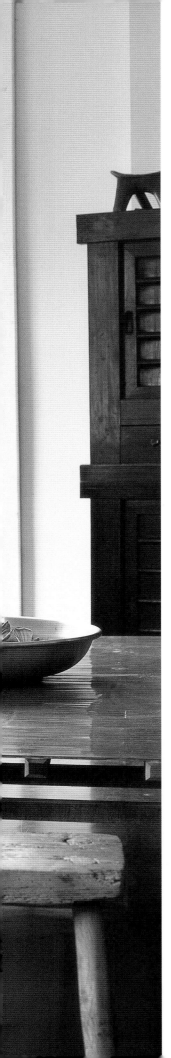

LEFT The owner left the windows bare so that light could flood in, and painted the walls in a pale, neutral shade, to offset his mixture of craft objects and artifacts from around the globe. The sofa and coffee table were designed and made by Sam Miller; the patterned velvet pillows are by textile designer Georgina von Etzdorf.

RIGHT The wooden doors were specially made for the space, and the raw mahogany stairposts were bought from a builder's yard. The platinum photographs are just two among many artworks in the flat by friends of the owner.

ESSENTIAL COMFORT

Once a series of dark, poky rooms, this north London apartment has been opened up to create a flowing series of airy spaces that are filled with light. Peace, calm, and quiet were the owner's aims—and despite its urban setting, the apartment has these qualities in abundance, thanks to its combination of restful colors, tactile natural materials, and evocative handmade objects.

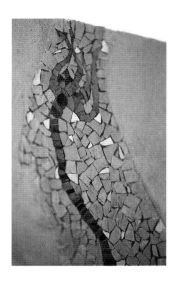

LEFT The decorative backsplash behind the kitchen sink was made by mosaic artist Catherine Parkinson.

RIGHT A rudimentary but attractive dining table is the main focus of the L-shaped dining room. It was made by a local carpenter from "bits of wood." The chairs came from a cricket pavilion in the East End of London. The set of glasses are Victorian.

FAR RIGHT, ABOVE AND BELOW The interior designer who owns this flat is not a fan of built-in kitchens; his kitchen is composed of a simple series of open wooden shelves, arranged around a large butler's sink, with all utensils on display.

The word "craft" has acquired some unfortunate connotations, evoking images of crocheted doilies and kitsch dolls—which is a shame, because craft objects can be the most elegant, spiritual, and individual pieces in a home. This flat's owner, an interior designer, is firmly in the craft-lovers' camp although, sensitive to the nuances of public perception, he prefers to describe his objects as "handmade." As he puts it: "I don't want to live with a load of designer furniture. It's lovely to have things that are one-offs, to give your space an identity of its own."

Before introducing these very personal pieces, the owner had to gut and remodel the entire space. It was in a desperate state when he bought it: a rabbit warren of tiny rooms, with orange walls and swirly carpets. But, thanks to its corner site and great views over a park, it had an abundance of light. He opened the place out so that one room flowed into another, and added another floor for a bedroom and bathroom, with a pitched ceiling "so it's like waking up in a tent."

His next step was to cover the floors in shiny black rubber tiling—inspired by Richard Wilson's oil installation in London's Saatchi Gallery. The

thick blackness of the flooring is very calming, and provides a neutral base against which to offset an eclectic mix of furnishings. The owner's aim was to create the atmosphere of a beach house—warm in winter, cool in summer— with a relaxed, colonial feel. "I love the idea of having a holiday home in London," he says.

Then came the furniture, predominantly made of wood, raw and tactile, its grain, knots, cracks, and flaws shown off in full glory. The owner's

LEFT The natural colors and intricate patterning of the mosaic fire surround are complemented by the shiny rubber flooring found throughout the flat. The classic armchair, slipcovered in white cotton, was a gift from a friend, and the mobile in the corner is made of driftwood from Mexico.

THIS PAGE "My big passion is things that are handmade," says the owner. Here, the carefully crafted fire surround, which was made from subtly colored stone by Catherine Parkinson, is complemented by an antique wooden neck pillow, which he bought in Hong Kong.

LEFT The interior designer who own the flat says that sleeping in his attic, with its sloping ceiling and skylight, is like "waking up in a tent." His carpenter crafted the wooden cupboards; the owner and a friend made the striped cotton quilt, and the line was sold to Browns in London and Collette, a Parisian shop .

RIGHT At the opposite end of the room is a vast Edwardian rolltop bathtub reclaimed from a demolition site. The modern egg-shaped light in the corner casts a soft glow at night.

BELOW The downstairs powder room is simply fitted out with a huge square ceramic sink and a series of old mirrors.

Almost everything in this interior designer's apartment is handmade, most of it by friends—and those objects that are not handmade are either antique, retro, or recycled.

friend Sam Miller designed and made the sofa, coffee table, and desk. The mahogany stairposts came from a builder's yard; the dining chairs were from an East End cricket pavilion, and a carpenter made the bedroom cupboards.

Another friend, mosaic artist Catherine Parkinson, made a fire surround in which the colors and textures of the material combine in a Missoni-esque fusion—quite the most stylish mosaic that you are ever likely to find. Other friends contributed art works, sculptures, a set of Victorian glasses, and a fabric bowl, and the owner added bits and pieces picked up from travels to the Far East, creating an intricate layering of periods, places, and personalities.

Finally, adding yet another dimension to this already highly sensory space, he sprayed subtle Italian scent, sprinkled potpourri, and burned incense, creating a truly personal ambience and adding even deeper emotional appeal. As he says: "It's all about creating a space in which you can feel better about your life."

RAW NATURE

When space and light are what you want, it pays to be bold and determined. In this Victorian row house, for example, practically all the ground-floor internal walls were taken out, as were the small sash windows, and replaced with a wall of folding glass doors that make the courtyard garden an extension of the living room. A confident mixture of tough materials and robust furniture makes this a home that's both comfortable and individual.

There can't be many city homes where you are awoken by the sound of mooing cows. From the bedroom window of Emma Wilson's row house, you can see not only cows, but also sheep, goats, and even geese, although she's just yards from one of North London's trendiest shopping areas. It's a city farm that provides the rural soundtrack, but inside the house there's a natural tendency, too. Wilson, who used to be a florist and now rents out her home for photographic and film shoots, has taken robust materials—distressed leather, raw wood, and bashed concrete—and used them in a way that is bold, fresh, and invigorating.

First, she had to alter the layout of what was a typical Victorian property, with a narrow entrance hall, front and back parlors, and small sash windows. "I wanted it to be very open and roomy, and to be able to feel space and light," she says. Having taken out the downstairs walls, so that the front door opens into one huge living space, she then installed a wall of folding metal-and-glass doors that lead straight into the small

LEFT Emma Wilson installed the folding metal-and-glass doors in place of a small sash window, allowing light to flood into the living room. The curvy dining table, which incorporates an old blackboard in its surface, was made by designer Ben Huggins.

ABOVE RIGHT The kitchen work surface was also constructed by Huggins. He cast the concrete with a U-shape to hold a sink made of waterproof supele wood.

RIGHT Rough, raw wood and metal dominate the kitchen. Unconventional open shelving is used to store dishes, and a collection of old enamel pitchers, found at flea markets, hangs from a row of hooks.

LEFT An old hospital trolley, which was found in an antique store, serves as a functional dressing table in Emma Wilson's bedroom.

RIGHT This 1940s pine chest—another antique-store find—is used to store clothes.

BELOW The bathroom is painted a quiet shade of duck-egg blue. The fixtures successfully mix old and new, with an inset butler's sink teamed with a minimal Vola faucet and sleek wall-to-wall mirroring.

Robust and tactile materials—such as distressed leather, raw wood, and bashed concrete—are used in a way that is bold, fresh, and invigorating.

courtyard garden. She covered the walls in white plaster and stripped the paint off every surface, from doors and shelves to window frames and staircases, revealing the natural patina of whatever was underneath. Old fire surrounds were ripped out, too, to be replaced by simple holes in the wall, but the original wooden floors and baseboards were left. "The more worn everything is the better I like it," she says.

The choice of furniture follows the same ethos. Sometimes antique, sometimes reclaimed junk, sometimes made to Wilson's design, it is always solid, honest, and straightforward, and often impressively sized. The large mirrors, for example, make a marvelous feature, and reflect yet more light into the airy space. In the kitchen, a massive wooden block forms the top of a salvaged butcher's block, while monumental railroad ties serve as a coffee table, and scaffolding poles as a bed frame.

In this confident, country-meets-city home, even the plant pots are gutsy—an old metal pail sits on the coffee table, overflowing with herbs. Warm, comfortable, and inviting it may be, but this is no place for delicate little flowers.

BELOW From Emma Wilson's uncluttered bedroom, a spiral staircase leads to a mezzanine-level office. Absence of color and pattern gives the room, as elsewhere in the house, a profoundly restful feel—aided by the background sound of animals from the city farm across the road. The scaffolding bed was made by a company called Twelve, and is kept utterly simple with plain white bedlinen. The lamp came from an antique store, and Wilson picked up the lovely old wooden window shutters at a fair.

TALES OF THE UNEXPECTED

ABOVE In a corner of the garden room, rows of plants in pots have been carefully arranged around a pair of antique gilt mirrors notable for their foxed patina.

ABOVE RIGHT On the top floor, a tiny wooden door opens out onto a decked terrace. The basket seats date from the 1950s.

OPPOSITE All the walls have been whitewashed to make the house light and airy throughout. This bright garden room leads onto an upstairs terrace. Above the curly-metal garden chair hangs a pretty French chandelier, with real candles.

London's East End is full of areas that ache with history. One such is Spitalfields, which became known for its market, licensed in 1638; then, in the later 17th century, for its influx of French Protestant refugees, many of them skilled weavers. Open fields were fast covered by streets lined by grand houses. Over the years, successive waves of immigrants have made Spitalfields their home. Old and new, global cultures, and dynamic enterprise: a unique mix that gives the place its rich and vibrant character.

Pass through the front door of some Georgian houses in Spitalfields and it's like stepping back in time, so sensitively have they been restored. In Ann Shore's house, however, it's not so much a question of going back in time as of stepping out of time. While certainly not modern, the house is not "period" either, nor is it typically British—the objects that surround you might come from Denmark, Morocco, India, or Bali, and could be ancient, antique, 20th-century classics, or even made last week.

Shore, who owns a shop, designs clothes and jewelry, and styles fashion and interiors, has worked hard to create a look that is authentic in itself but not doggedly 18th century. When she bought the house, it had already been partly restored, but not much of it to her taste. The kitchen, for example, was lovely, but had to go. "It just looked 'done,'" she says. "I can't stand anything precious or fussed over, so it all came out and became much more basic." So basic, in fact, that she cooks on a 1930s Aga, washes her dishes by hand, and has left her copper pipework exposed and unpainted. There is no central heating—she lights fires instead—and electrical fixtures are as unobtrusive as possible; candlelight is always the first option.

OPPOSITE, LEFT The white fireplace looks like an abstract sculpture. Afghan bowls and an African food carrier stand on the mantelpiece.

MAIN PICTURE Two worn and comfortable leather are surrounded by an eclectic mixture of objects, including Balinese baskets, pots and bowls from India, Afghanistan, and Morocco, and a pile of textiles from India.

LEFT Another large foxed mirror dominates the bedroom.

BELOW The daring mix of objects includes a 1970s chair placed in front of a cupboard containing an African comb, Indian mud pots, and a Filipino tamarind-seed necklace.

ABOVE A montage of intriguing monochromatic images adorns the fridge. Above the sink is a wirework plate drainer.

LEFT The kitchen is functional but basic. The owner replaced the African slate floor with "more honest" York stone flags. She does all her cooking on a 1930s Aga, which offers a cosy spot for her Siamese cat, Tunes. Hanging from a cupboard handle is a gourd that has been made into a carrier.

RIGHT This space on the top floor is used variously as a place to work or sit, or as a spare bedroom. An old sari has been thrown over the 1930s Heal's chair, while in the background a half-stripped cabinet displays jewellery from Africa and India.

Like a stage, a still-life, or a frame from a film, everything is placed in order to create fascinating vignettes, combining colors, textures, and forms in intriguing and interesting ways.

"The underlying theme is to be very natural and light," says Ann Shore. "It's a pure backdrop on which to layer things as much or as little as I like. In spring, for instance, the house is very light and bright, while in the winter I tend to warm it up a little by getting out the rugs, lighting fires, burning candles, and so on."

This element of constant, fuss-free change, like a narrative unfolding, is central to Shore's philosophy. Her store, which began life in this house, is called Story, and contains eclectic, unpretentious, beautiful things that come from all sorts of places and periods.

Everything in Ann Shore's home is arranged to create fascinating vignettes, mixing colors, textures, and forms in intriguing ways. The arrangements are carefully done, yet appear casual and natural. Her skill lies in combining apparently disparate objects and making them work together; what links them is a strong visual aesthetic that enjoys the unconventional as much as the traditional and celebrates the worn,

RIGHT AND BELOW
Shore collects shoes,
seeing them as works of
art as much as things to
wear. The gold slippers
are 15 years old.

FAR RIGHT Her work
table is functional and
plain, but beautiful in its
simplicity; the chair is
1970s plywood, covered
in brown velvet.

BELOW RIGHT An
Indian throw with gilt
edging and embroidery
covers the futon bed.

OPPOSITE This
dramatic dress, its bold
pattern a vivid contrast to
the plain white fireplace,
is a vintage piece picked
up from a collector; it
probably dates from
the late 1960s.

the old, the battered, and the used. "I love things that have a patina, some sort of wear and tear," she says. "It shows they have a life, and means that you don't have to be afraid to use them." It could be a leather armchair or a pair of 1950s spike heels; a woven African basket or a pretty French chandelier—each piece has an intrinsic, and very individual, attraction.

In common with her aversion to the mod cons of 21st-century life, Ann Shore favours modest, environmentally friendly materials. Her floors are stone or wood, her walls whitewashed, and her windows bare—except for the occasional blind or fragment of antique lace. Any interventions are minimal. The fireplaces, for example, have all been painted white, but Shore did not use specialist paint, just ordinary limewash. "So what if it rusts? I can either paint them again or leave them." Such a relaxed attitude demonstrates the effortless ease with which this owner makes sure that every element in her home acts out its place in her story perfectly.

ROSS BLECKNER

PETER LINDBERGH

JAZZ

PICTURE CREDITS

a = above, **b** = below, **c** = center, **l** = left, **r** = right, *ph* = photographer

Endpapers *ph* Ray Main; page **1** *ph* James Morris; **2** *ph* Simon Upton/Carol Reid's apartment in Paris; **3** *ph* Brian Leonard; **4–5** *ph* Ray Main; **6** *ph* Debi Treloar; **7** *ph* Chris Everard; **8l** & **9** *ph* Francesca Yorke/Valerie Rossmore's garden in London; **8r** *ph* Chris Everard; **10–11** *ph* Chris Everard/Sig.ra Venturini's apartment in Milan; **12l** *ph* Chris Everard/Philippe Model's apartment in Paris; **12br** *ph* Chris Everard/an apartment in Milan designed by Nicoletta Marazza; **12–13a** *ph* Andrew Wood/Mary Shaw's Sequana apartment in Paris; **13a** *ph* Chris Everard; 13b *ph* Chris Everard; **14–21** *ph* Chris Everard/Philippe Model's apartment in Paris; **22–29** *ph* Chris Everard/Gentucca Bini's apartment in Milan; **30–37** *ph* Chris Everard/Eric De Queker's apartment in Antwerp; **38–43** *ph* Chris Everard/Sig.ra Venturini's apartment in Milan; **44–49** *ph* Jan Baldwin/Interior Designer Didier Gomez's apartment in Paris; **50–57** *ph* Alan Williams/Warner Johnson's apartment in New York designed by Edward Cabot of Cabot Design Ltd.; **58–59** *ph* James Morris/Skywood House near London designed by Graham Phillips; **60l** *ph* James Morris/a house in London designed by Alan Power; **60br** *ph* Ray Main/central London apartment designed by Ben Kelly Design, 1999; **60–61a** *ph* Chris Everard/an apartment in New York designed by Gabellini Associates; **61a** *ph* Simon Upton/designed by Brian Alfred Murphy; **61b** *ph* Andrew Wood/Roger and Suzy Black's apartment in London designed by Johnson Naylor; **62–69** Johanne Riss' house in Brussels: **62–63** *ph* Catherine Gratwicke; **64–65** *ph* Andrew Wood; **66** & **67al** *ph* Catherine Gratwicke; **67ar&b**, **68–69** *ph* Andrew Wood; **70–77** designed by Ian Chee of VX design & architecture www.vxdesign.com/ ianchee@vxdesign.com: all *ph* Chris Everard, except **72br** *ph* Thomas Stewart; **78–87** *ph* Simon Upton/José de Yturbe's home in Mexico City; **88–95** *ph* Andrew Wood/Brian Johnson's apartment in London designed by Johnson Naylor; **96–103** *ph* Jan Baldwin/ designer Chester Jones' house in London; **104–11** *ph* James Morris/the Lew House, originally designed by Richard Neutra in 1958, architect and contractor Marmol Radziner + Associates, Architecture and Construction; **112–19** *ph* Chris Everard/Ou Baholyodhin & Erez Yardeni's Penthouse, Highpoint, London; **120–21** & **122al** *ph* Alan Williams/interior designer John Barman's own apartment in New York; **122bl** *ph* Thomas Stewart/Neil Bingham's house in Blackheath, London; **122br** *ph* Alan Williams/the architect Voon Wong's own apartment in London; **122–23a** *ph* Andrew Wood/Chelsea Loft apartment in New York, designed by The Moderns; **123a** *ph* Chris Everard; **123b** *ph* Andrew Wood/Kurt Bredenbeck's apartment at the Barbican, London; **124–31** *ph* Ray Main/Evan Snyderman's house in Brooklyn; **132–39** *ph* Andrew Wood/an apartment in the San Remo on the Upper West Side of Manhattan, designed by John L. Stewart and Michael D'Arcy of SIT; **140–47** *ph* Andrew Wood/John Cheim's apartment in New York; **148–55** *ph* Chris Everard/an apartment in London designed by Jo Hagan of Use Architects; **156l** *ph* Chris Everard; **156–61** *ph* Andrew Wood/Kurt Bredenbeck's apartment at the Barbican, London; **162–63** *ph* Tom Leighton; **164al** & **164–65a** *ph* Catherine Gratwicke/Laura Stoddart's apartment in London; **164bl** *ph* Catherine Gratwicke/photographer Marie-Pierre Morel's house in Paris, designed by François Muracciole; **164br** *ph* Ray Main/Jonathan Leitersdorf's apartment in New York designed by Jonathan Leitersdorf/Just Design Ltd; **165a** *ph* Ray Main; **165b** *ph* Jan Baldwin/Emma Wilson's house in London; **166–71** *ph* Tom Leighton/two lofts in the old center of Amsterdam of Annette Brederode, painter & dealer/collector of antiques and "brocante" and Aleid Röntgen-Brederode, landscape architect; **172–79** Carol Reid's apartment in Paris: **172** *ph* Polly Wreford; **173** *ph* Simon Upton; **174** *ph* Polly Wreford; **174–75** *ph* Simon Upton; **175a&b** *ph* Polly Wreford; **176–77** & **177a** *ph* Simon Upton; **177b** *ph* Polly Wreford; **178–79** all *ph* Polly Wreford; **180–89** photographer Marie-Pierre Morel's house in Paris, designed by François Muracciole: **180–81**, **182a** & **182–83b** *ph* Ray Main; **183a** *ph* Catherine Gratwicke; **184al** *ph* Ray Main; **184bl**, **184–85** & **185ar** *ph* Catherine Gratwicke; **185br** & **186–89** all *ph* Ray Main; **190–97** *ph* Andrew Wood/Jones Miller studio in New York designed by Giuseppe Lignano and Ada Tolla of LOT/EK Architecture; **198–205** *ph* Jan Baldwin: **198** furniture made by Sam Miller; **200–203** mosaics designed by Catherine Parkinson; **206–11** *ph* Jan Baldwin/Emma Wilson's house in London; **212–19** *ph* Polly Wreford/Ann Shore's former home in London.

ARCHITECTS AND DESIGNERS

whose work is featured in this book

OU BAHOLYODHIN STUDIO

1ST FLOOR
12 GREATOREX STREET
LONDON E1 5NF
+44 (0)20 7426 0666
www.ou-b.com
Pages **112–19.**

JOHN BARMAN INC.
INTERIOR DESIGN & DECORATION

500 PARK AVENUE
NEW YORK
NY 10022
212 838 9443
www.johnbarman.com
Pages **120–21, 122al.**

ANNETTE BREDERODE
PAINTER, ANTIQUE
DEALER/COLLECTOR AND
ALEID RÖNTGEN-BREDERODE
LANDSCAPE ARCHITECT

LIJNBAANSGRACHT 56D
1015 GS AMSTERDAM
HOLLAND
Pages **166–71.**

CABOT DESIGN LTD
INTERIOR DESIGN

1925 SEVENTH AVENUE,
SUITE 71
NEW YORK
NY10026
212 222 9488
eocabot@aol.com
Pages **50–57.**

IAN CHEE
VX DESIGN & ARCHITECTURE

www.vxdesign.com
ianchee@vxdesign.com
Pages **70–77.**

SANDY DAVIDSON DESIGN

1505 VIEWSITE TERRACE
LOS ANGELES
CA 90069
sandsandd@aol.com
Front jacket.

ERIC DE QUEKER
DQ-DESIGN IN MOTION

KONINKLIJKELAAN 44
2600 BERCHAM
BELGIUM
Pages **30–37.**

GABELLINI ASSOCIATES

665 BROADWAY
SUITE 706
NEW YORK
NY 10012
212 388 1700
Pages **60–61a.**

DIDIER GOMEZ
INTERIOR DESIGNER

ORYGOMEZ
15 RUE HENRI HEINE
75016 PARIS
FRANCE
+ 33 01 44 30 8823
orygomez@free.fr
Back jacket above right,
Pages **44–49.**

WILLIAM R. HEFNER AIA
WILLIAM HEFNER ARCHITECT LLC

5820 WILSHIRE BOULEVARD
SUITE 601
LOS ANGELES
CA 90036
323 931 1365
www.williamhefner.com
Front jacket.

JOHNSON NAYLOR

13 BRITTON STREET
LONDON EC1M 5SX
+44 (0)20 7490 8885
brian.johnson@johnsonnaylor.co.uk
Pages **61b, 88–95.**

CHESTER JONES LTD
INTERIOR DESIGNERS

240 BATTERSEA PARK ROAD
LONDON SW11 4NG
+44 (0)20 7498 2717
chester.jones@virgin.net
Pages **96–103.**

BEN KELLY DESIGN

10 STONEY STREET
LONDON SE1 9AD
+44 (0)20 7378 8116
bkduk@dircon.co.uk
Page **60br.**

JUST DESIGN LTD

80 FIFTH AVENUE
18TH FLOOR
NEW YORK
NY 10011
212 243 6544
wbp@angel.net
Back jacket below,
Page **164br.**

LOT/EK ARCHITECT

55 LITTLE WEST 12TH STREET
NEW YORK
NY 10014
212 255 9326
Pages **190–197.**

NICOLETTA MARAZZA

VIA G. MORONE, 8
20121 MILAN
ITALY
+39 2 7601 4482
Page **12br.**

**MARMOL & RADZINER +
ASSOCIATES,
ARCHITECTURE +
CONSTRUCTION**

2902 NEBRASKA AVENUE
SANTA MONICA
CA 90404
310 264 1814
www.marmol-radziner.com
Pages **104–111.**

**SAM MILLER
FURNITURE MAKER**

+44 (0)20 8878 3850
sammiller@i12.com
Page **198.**

THE MODERNS

900 BROADWAY
SUITE 903
NEW YORK
NY 10003
212 387 8852
moderns@aol.com
Pages **122–23a.**

PHILIPPE MODEL

33 PLACE DU
   MARCHÉ ST. HONORÉ
75001 PARIS
FRANCE
+33 1 4296 8902
Pages **12l, 14–21.**
Decoration, home furnishings,
and coverings.

**FRANÇOIS MURACCIOLE
ARCHITECT & DESIGN**

54 RUE DE MONTREUIL
75011 PARIS
FRANCE
+33 1 43 71 33 03
francois.muracciole@libertysurf.fr
Pages **164bl, 180–89.**
Houses, offices, shops,
furniture, and more.

**BAM CONSTRUCTION/
DESIGN INC
BRIAN ALFRED MURPHY
ARCHITECT**

150 W. CHANNEL ROAD
SANTA MONICA
CA 90402
3104590955
Page **61a.**

**CATHERINE PARKINSON
MOSAICS**

+44 (0)20 8964 1945
Pages **200–203.**

**GRAHAM PHILLIPS RIBA
ARCHITECT**

Pages **58–59.**

**ALAN POWER
ARCHITECTS**

5 HAYDENS PLACE
LONDON W11 1LY
+44 (0)20 7229 9375
Page **60l.**

**JOHANNE RISS
STYLIST, DESIGNER &
FASHION DESIGNER**

35 PLACE DU NOUVEAU
   MARCHÉ AUX GRAENS
1000 BRUSSELS
BELGIUM
+32 2 513 0900
www.johanneriss.com
Pages **62–69.**

SEQUANA

64 AVENUE DE LA MOTTE
PICQUET
75015 PARIS
FRANCE
+33 1 45 66 58 40
sequana@wanadoo.fr
Pages **12–13a.**

**JOHN L. STEWART
SIT, LLC**

113–115 BANK STREET
NEW YORK
NY 10014
212 620 777
JLSCollection@aol.com
Pages **132–39.**

STORY

4 WILKES STREET
SPITALFIELDS
E1 6QF
+44 (0)20 7377 0313
story@btconnect.com
Pages **212–19.**
Personal selection of old and
new furniture and accessories
(afternoons only).

USE ARCHITECTS

11 NORTHBURGH STREET
LONDON EC1V 0AH
+44 (0)20 7251 5559
use.arch@virgin.net
Pages **148–55.**

EMMA WILSON

London home available for
photographic shoots:
www.45crossleyst.com
and Moroccan home available
for holiday lets:
www.castlesinthesand.com
Pages **165b, 206–11.**

VOON WONG ARCHITECTS

UNIT 27
1 STANNARY STREET
LONDON SE11 4AD
+44 (0)20 75870116
voon@dircon.co.uk
Page **122br.**

EREZ YARDENI STUDIO

FUNCTION 1ST FLOOR
12 GREATOREX STREET
LONDON E1 5NF
+44 (0)20 7426 0666
Pages **112–19.**

**JOSÉ DE YTURBE
DE YTURBE ARQUITECTOS**

PATRIOTISMO 13 (4° PISO)
LOMAS DE BARRILACO
MEXICO 11010 DF
00 525 540 368
deyturbe@infosel.net.mx
Pages **78–87.**

INDEX

Page numbers in *italic* denote captions and illustrations.